BOUDICA'S
LAST
STAND

D1484245

Dial

BOUDICA'S LAST STAND

BRITAIN'S REVOLT AGAINST ROME AD 60-61

JOHN WAITE

This book is dedicated to my two sons, Robert and Marcus.

Also to the memory of Brian Archer.
A true father figure whose encouragement and understanding
nurtured my love of the ancient world.
The artwork I have completed for this book is, I hope, a fitting and
lasting tribute to Bry, a very special man who will be always be greatly
missed and fondly remembered.

Front cover portrait: © Photofrenetic/ Alamy

First published in 2007
This edition published in 2011

The History Press
The Mill, Brimscombe Port
Stroud, Gloucestershire, GL5 2QG
www.thehistorypress.co.uk

British Library Cataloguing in Publication Data.
A catalogue record for this book is available from the British Library.

ISBN 978 0 7524 5909 7

Typesetting and origination by The History Press
Printed in Great Britain
Manufacturing managed by Jellyfish Print Solutions Ltd

CONTENTS

Introduction

Nearly 2,000 years ago, in the fenlands of eastern Britain, a series of events began to unfold which would eventually see the widow of a minor client ruler become so celebrated that today she ranks amongst the great names of world history. Her story is so stirring and compelling in its allure that many writers, chroniclers, and commentators in the centuries since that time have been unable to resist adding their own contribution to the wealth of material that now exists on the subject. Everything from biographies to films, plays to academic titles, paintings and sculptures, have all been produced which serve to keep alive the story of a long-ago native uprising and the woman who led it. The revolt is viewed by us in many ways; it can be told as a story of the oppressed rising up to rid themselves of tyranny, or perhaps as a straightforward tale of bloody revenge for the sufferance of gross injustices. But however one chooses to view this story it is certain that, had the revolt succeeded, Rome would have lost its grip on Britain and the island nation we know today could be a very different place indeed.

It would not be too unrealistic to suggest that anyone possessed of a little knowledge of Britain's rich history will have heard of Boudica or Boadicea, as she is perhaps more commonly known. The now iconic

Queen of the Iceni is the historical embodiment and epitome of so many aspects of that unique spirit which defines the island race of the British people. Her story also speaks to us of so many things that the British people of today hold sacred, such as our love of independence, our resistance to oppression and, then as now, the tenacity we still display in the fearsome fighting spirit of a small nation defending itself against many a determined and powerful aggressor. Such values could be regarded as part of the very DNA which characterises the British identity, and which ultimately forged a nation that has successfully repelled every serious attempt to invade it since the arrival of the Normans in 1066. Today Boudica's light burns as bright as it ever did, and although the intervening years have obscured many of the facts relating to both the queen and the revolt, that obscurity does not appear to have been a barrier to our desire to understand these things. Certainly, this book too is a product of that enduring enthusiasm, but perhaps it is now time to approach the story from a less well-examined angle.

Today there is a wealth of information about Boudica, tirelessly pieced together from what amounts to little more than fragmentary evidence. Work has been produced on both the queen as an individual and on the cult of personality that is Boudica. Despite the wealth of material produced, there is little we can say for certain about the real Boudica and the life she lived. Much of the material that we consider to be 'in depth' must really be regarded more as informed speculation because, other than the very brief mentions she receives in classical records, there are no contemporary works that detail Boudica or any of the significant stages of her life. The purpose of this work, therefore, is not to attempt an in-depth analysis or seek to build a profile of the queen herself. Instead, it will re-assess the documentary and archaeological evidence in order to explore the mechanics of the revolt itself. By reviewing the tactics used both by Boudica and her Roman opponent Paulinus it will seek to place some new ideas into the arena of discussion, including a fresh theory on that most tantalising of questions relating to the revolt, that of where the final battle actually took place.

The mists of nearly 2,000 years of time have shrouded the facts of what really happened when Queen Boudica, her tribe and her allies rose up in a brief but bloody rebellion against Roman oppression in AD 61. However, as we have already touched upon, this relative obscurity has never stood in the way of generations of study and conjecture on the subject. Our knowledge of many of the key events building up to and during the various phases of the uprising is now reasonably clear, but that recurrent question concerning the actual location of Boudica's last great battle still begs an answer.

There have been many suggestions forwarded as to where that battlefield may be, and the various locations that have been proposed cover a wide area of Britain, from North Wales to Epping Forest. These sites have been mooted by anyone from eminent historians and archaeologists to ordinary local people convinced that the folklore of their area holds the answer. A good example of a suggested site would be Gop Hill in Flintshire. The location is backed up by some of that very same local folklore which has endured amongst the local population for generations, while a wealth of physical clues, such as Iron Age burial mounds and ancient stone cairns, circumstantially help to perpetuate the idea that here is where it all ended. One nineteenth-century Welsh writer, Owen Morien Morgan, put forward the theory that the battle took place on the Rhuddlan Plain and that Boudica later died in Rhyl. Indeed, North Wales has an abundance of folk stories and sites to which people refer when claiming that the battle and burial site are local to their region. Certainly, there could be a no more appealing version of the tale to stimulate the more romantic side of our nature than the idea of the great warrior queen contradicting the versions penned by Roman historians and living out her days in peace. Even if it is a fanciful notion, it is still a temptation to think of her safely hidden away from her enemies in the rolling, misty lands of wild tribes that stubbornly refused ever to capitulate fully to the will of Rome. A safe haven at the very edge of the empire for a queen who will always be remembered as a very formidable and ultimately worthy foe.

Some suggest that Boudica fought her last battle in the counties of Warwickshire or Northamptonshire, while others champion the somewhat bizarre claim that her body now rests under a platform of Kings Cross train station in London. There exist many more regions throughout the southern half of Britain which have suggested that theirs is the only true battle site, and that Boudica never even saw Wales. And so it would seem that everyone with a valid theory is eager to claim ownership of a key piece of the story, championing their own region as the true host to such historically significant events. Were they ever able to present solid evidence to support the claim then at last the ghost of Boudica could be laid to rest.

A possible spin-off for the region that finally is able to claim ownership of the battlefield could lie with it making the somewhat grandiose claim of being the very seat of the society that the British have become today. Ambitious though it might be, such a boast could indeed be made with some conviction, due to the fact that the Roman Emperor at the time of the revolt, Nero, had already seriously considered pulling out of Britain. But, as the Roman historian Suetonius records in *The Twelve Caesars*, Nero finally decided to maintain his grip on the province in preference to abandoning it, 'because such a decision may have reflected on the glory won by his adoptive father, Claudius'.

There can therefore be little doubt that if the fortunes of war had swung the other way and Gaius Suetonius Paulinus, the Roman governor of Britain at the time, had not prevailed, the Roman administration would have suffered a catastrophic defeat at the hands of Boudica. Roman control of the province would have been totally lost and Nero, dispensing with the previous nostalgic sentiments for the late lamented Claudius and lacking in expansionist ambitions anyway, would probably have made no effort to reclaim it, choosing instead to turn his back on the troublesome island lying at the very edge of the empire. The resultant restoration of the previously established insular Celtic tribal culture would then have meant that we would possibly now be enjoying a very different way of life to the one we lead today.

Of all the suggested locations, the one that is most commonly favoured by modern scholars and historians, and one championed by the late Dr Graham Webster, is Mancetter in Warwickshire, a small, mainly residential area on the edge of the market town of Atherstone in the north of the county. Dr Webster offers us the meticulous evidence of his own archaeological work and that of other notable scholars and archaeological groups working in the area of the Warwickshire town. The result of this collective work is then supported by his comparisons of the modern topography to what we know about the battle site from the description recorded in the near-contemporary classical account of the engagement. Regrettably, although Dr Webster's arguments for Mancetter being the battle site are strong, they are not conclusive beyond doubt. As shall be evidenced later on in this work, the suggested location contains certain problematic elements which indicate that the site is actually an unlikely one. The plain fact of the matter is that the evidence contained within the known classical sources is insufficient on its own to be able to determine the exact location of the site. This means that until definitive and indisputable archaeological evidence is provided, one theory will have just as much merit as the next.

So what of that much sought-after evidence that will finally serve to tie the whole story down? Well, there is a very real possibility that nothing conclusive will ever be found. Such a battlefield would leave very few permanent features to assist in its identification. No classical writings survive that suggest the Roman forces prepared their positions with any defensive structures prior to the arrival of Boudica's army. That said, just because the chroniclers failed to mention this certainly does not mean that Paulinus did not in fact set about preparing a specifically chosen position, given that the Roman legionaries were excellent engineers and any advantage that could have been seized no doubt would have been. However, as Dr Webster once pointed out, had Paulinus not made these preparations to the chosen ground then the very best anyone could expect to find would be military small finds and perhaps mass graves around the site of the battle.

This is certainly easier said than done, considering that if the site is not buried under buildings then it is likely to be in a more rural location, perhaps with any evidence either obliterated by intensive modern farming techniques or obscured under evidence of medieval ridge and furrow sites. Certainly, whilst the discovery of any surviving evidence would be invaluable, the task of locating it would require an incredible amount of time and money. Unfortunately, these are two commodities that many of today's archaeologists do not enjoy in abundance.

In view of the fact that several plausible theories exist with regard to the battle site, it is worth asking oneself whether yet another theory is going to be well received, or whether it may just be regarded as yet another round of informed speculation, vaguely interesting perhaps but not really worthy of any serious consideration. Although it is certainly true that many books exist on the subject of Boudica and the revolt, if the latter attitude was the case then we would be failing in our obligation to remain objective. More positive is the view that we should seek to examine carefully any credible propositions that are newly forwarded on the topic. One must always bear in mind that history has frequently been rewritten, both in light of new discoveries and through re-examination of what we previously understood to be the facts. The primary purpose of this book, therefore, is not necessarily to try to discredit alternative theories but to impartially strip the events back to their beginnings and rebuild the story piece by piece, examining the history, the key players, the events themselves and the advantages that could have resulted from certain actions or strategies. We need to re-examine the roots of the rebellion, and look closely at Boudica's possible motivations beyond that of bloody revenge. We should closely examine the question of whether there was the possibility of a higher agenda and what the implications of such an agenda may have been, both to the province of Britannia and to the Roman governor Paulinus. To him alone fell the daunting task of hurriedly devising an emergency stratagem that would halt the deadly tide of mass rebellion and, ultimately, restore the rule of Roman law.

The foundation of our understanding of those events has been based on the writings of two classical historians, Publius Cornelius Tacitus and Cassius Dio. As our best, near contemporary, sources of evidence, they provide a basic summary of the key events. We should remember, however, that these accounts were written years after the revolt and by people who were not even eyewitnesses to the actual events, building their descriptions instead by relying wholly on the accounts of others. The modern reader also has to be aware that there could also have been certain personal agendas in existence which the ancient authors themselves took the opportunity to satisfy, using their writing as a vehicle to achieve those goals. We must therefore be careful about how we interpret the information that they provide.

Tacitus's account is closest to a contemporary one, but he was only three or four years old at the time of these events and did not commit them to record until the end of the first century AD, around forty years later. It may be that much of what he had to say about the military history of early Roman Britain was learnt from his father-in-law, Gnaeus Julius Agricola, who, having seen military service in Britain, subsequently became governor of the province between AD 77 and 83. Agricola conducted many great campaigns during his time in military service and Tacitus meticulously recorded his father-in-law's exploits in a volume called, succinctly enough, the *Agricola*. However, Tacitus's work on the revolt may hold a definite bias concerning Agricola's recollections, especially given the fact that Agricola was serving as a young tribune on the staff of Paulinus when the revolt took place. He would no doubt have happily seized the opportunity to have both the glorious deeds of the Roman army, and his own exploits relating to the revolt, portrayed in the most favourable manner possible by his admiring historian son-in-law. Having said all that of Tacitus, it is his account of the revolt that should be considered the better version of those laid down by the only two known classical writers who have committed a description to posterity.

Born in the Greek province of Bythinia in AD 150, Cassius Dio, on the other hand, is writing well over a century after the revolt and is probably directly referencing from the writings of Tacitus, taking the original facts and embellishing them in the style of one of today's more sensationalist tabloid reporters. Although historically similar to the work of Tacitus, Dio's account contains liberal lacings of hype, sensationally spiced with graphic descriptions of killing and torture and then further bulked out with stirring but rambling speeches which, if nothing else, were contrived by the author to pour scorn on Nero, a man whom Dio clearly saw as one of Rome's worst emperors and who consequently deserved to be derided whenever the opportunity arose.

In setting down their respective accounts of the revolt, the most obvious problem that both Dio and Tacitus encountered was the amount of time that had elapsed between the events concerned and their being committed to record. Even today, in an age of information technology, historians can encounter problems in creating factually accurate accounts when researching historical events as recent as the Second World War. The Romans would have encountered exactly the same problems as we do today: the passage of time can rapidly muddy the waters as the writer attempts to retrieve the specific facts behind historic events.

Having embraced these accounts as the closest existing records of the events, it seems that modern exploration of the subject has mostly been contained by the limitations of the classical texts. Though the value of the accounts is clear, they are certainly not to be read casually. A close inspection of Tacitus's work will soon reveal inconsistencies and contradictions across his versions of events in different works such as the *Annals* and the *Agricola*. While it would be entirely unwise to disregard these accounts, perhaps it would be more sensible to treat them with a degree more caution than usual and expand our thinking to accommodate some fresher theories relating to the subject. Perchance, in light of these new theories, the quest to discover the truth may even take a new direction and ultimately spawn a new approach in the investigation of this spectacular piece of history. Ultimately, whatever direction the researchers of the future take, the real treasure will lay with that first exciting discovery of solid irrefutable evidence which, if it is out there waiting to be found, eventually leads us to the truth.

Wherever it may be.

1

THE PROTAGONISTS

BOUDICA, QUEEN OF THE ICENI

It has taken the best part of two millennia to mould the now stirring and iconic image of Boudica, one of the most famous queens in British history. A wealth of fact and speculation has merged over the years to forge an image of a truly enigmatic character, moulded together from so many different elements. Were it not for a brief flashpoint in time represented by the Boudican uprising, Boudica would probably be absent from popular British history. Had she not rose up and won the fame and notoriety that the ancient historians subsequently bestowed upon her then, like many other British tribal leaders, her name would have been absent from the traditional sources of evidence that today provide us with their names.

Even in the highly unlikely event that she could have succeeded to her dead husband's position as head of the Iceni, her role would likely have only been as a caretaker type of figurehead until the two daughters to whom Prasutagus had bequeathed half of his kingdom became old enough to rule in their own right. Boudica would doubtless have amounted to no more than an obscure name found on a coin, known only to specialist historians and academics.

The general public would never have got to hear of the deeds of this remarkable woman whose exploits firmly underpin the recorded history of the British Isles. Her name would be unknown to the generations of awed schoolchildren who have sat, open-mouthed, as the story of the fierce warrior queen has delighted and scared them over and over again. Obscurity, however, as we now well know, was the last thing that fate had in store for Boudica.

To the victor, Paulinus, went the accolade of saviour of the province of Britannia. However, to Boudica went the immortality bestowed by history, recorded for all posterity as the story of the oppressed underdog who rose up and fought for what she saw as a noble and righteous cause. Ironically, it is Roman writers who have preserved the story so well for us and to whom must fall the credit for elevating Boudica to the iconic status that she now holds. Because of the mighty Romans, her legend has echoed across time and her light burns as brightly now as it did nearly two millennia ago. In fact, in another ironical twist, it would be safe to say that, loser or not, her name is remembered by many more people than those who today recall the name of Paulinus, the man who eventually defeated her and saved Britannia from being lost to Rome.

In known records there exists nothing that could be considered an exact account of what Boudica actually looked like. The nearest description we have is more of a generic portrait of what people living in or around Rome understood the Celtic woman to look like. That account is given to us by Cassius Dio. However, given that Dio's style of writing is reliant on sensationalistic impact, often very flamboyant in style, and that his account was actually written over a century later, it would be pointless to consider the description as any more than speculative and perhaps an example of writer's licence, based on what was then known about the appearance of the people of Britain. As previously suggested, the description would have been a literary tool, formulated to impress the reader and build Boudica up as a more worthy opponent than just a mere woman:

In stature she was very tall, in appearance most terrifying, in the glance of her eye most fierce, and her voice was harsh; a great mass of the tawniest hair fell to her hips; around her neck was a large golden necklace; and she wore a tunic of divers colours over which a thick mantle was fastened with a brooch.

(Cassius Dio, *Roman Histories*, LXII)

In a few well-chosen words, Dio has conjured an image totally at odds with that of the typical benchmark on which the average Roman reader would base his perceptions of a woman. Polite Roman society would be used to seeing women of status and breeding with their heads respectfully covered and observant of the protocols of their social position. For a Roman woman, being publicly loud and outspoken and having one's head uncovered were the hallmarks of low society and ill repute.

Here then was this brash barbarian woman, loud mouthed and very much larger than life, having the outrageous temerity to question Roman rule and even going so far as to cause her tribe and neighbours to rise up in arms against that rule. The image this conveyed would be of a dangerous and cunning opponent, totally at odds with, and living beyond the conventions of, civilised society. If any justification were needed to make the reader feel that war against a woman was morally acceptable then this would go a long way to making it seem more palatable. As with Tacitus, Dio also mentions the fact that, although not the Roman way of war, in Britannia it was deemed acceptable for women to wage war on their foes. Readers of these works, being mostly the well-to-do of Roman society, would no doubt be astounded at the existence of such a foe and may even be minded to recall another occasion when Rome defeated Cleopatra, another foreign queen with high aspirations which ultimately required the Roman state to wage war on a woman. Besides any historical value the account would hold, the reader would view its content as further evidence of how mighty, all-conquering Rome could overcome the most exotic and dangerous of foes to prevail once more as undisputed masters of the world.

This concept of building your opponent into a physically daunting and fearful image is a literary device that both Dio and Tacitus have employed to good effect, especially when you combine the ferocity of the conjured image with the implication that the now demonised barbarian foe is also imbued with a high degree of eloquence and intelligence. Ever the sensationalist, Dio attributes to Boudica a lengthy and stirring address delivered to her rebel horde, both at the start of the uprising and when she finally confronts the army of Paulinus, deeply bemoaning the Roman foe, stoking up her army's thirst for revenge and invoking a sense of fair play and tribal pride in her assembled host as they wait to engage in battle. The contents of her speeches are strong and emotive words indeed, but, like the speech that Tacitus attributes to Calgacus the Caledonian before the Battle of Mons Graupius, Dio could never have known exactly what words she used to galvanise her forces and it should therefore be regarded as a wholly fictitious address, meant only to excite the emotions and steer the reader in the desired direction.

The typical Roman reader, then, having been carefully steered along the path that the author intended them to take, would be awed at the fact that such a powerful and intelligent foe had been defeated in far-flung foreign lands by the glorious imperial eagles of Rome, further strengthening their faith in the power of the Roman state and perhaps even maintaining a respectful fear of it. This then was how certain writers alluded to the greatness of Rome and how they delivered the classical image makeover given to Boudica. Ultimately this would be the way in which the foundations were laid for the manner in which we perceive her today.

This modern perception of Boudica's physical form is perhaps embodied best in the great bronze statue sculpted in the late Victorian era by Sir Thomas Thorneycroft and located on the Thames embankment at Westminster Bridge. The magnificent sculpture conveys all of the elements crucial to what we now understand of her character. As you view the statue from the front, it explodes with power and presence as a pair of mighty war horses pull a splendid chariot armed with bladed wheels and a defiant Boudica rides atop it, an avenging fury with arms outstretched and brandishing a spear. Just as this strong imagery conveys the power of the queen, so it also tells of the suffering endured by Boudica and her people as her two broken daughters, cruelly violated by the Romans, crouch down in the chariot, protected by their avenging mother as, immortalised now in bronze, they thunder eternally into battle by her side.

The more maternal image of Boudica as the protective mother has also been committed to sculpture and is rendered beautifully in the white marble statue now displayed in Cardiff's Civic Hall. Here there is no evidence of the warlike nature of the warrior queen; instead there exists a different perception which conveys the dignity, love and pride of a close family which has been deeply wronged. Boudica as the deeply slighted mother, having been publicly humiliated and flogged by Roman soldiers, pulls her ravished daughters into the protection of her skirts and stands proud and erect. In contrast to Thorneycroft's chariot queen, this sculpture suggests a more passive act of defiance towards her Roman tormentors. The simple, economical way in which the image is rendered still holds a defiant undertone, but it is less graphic and obvious than the image provided by Thorneycroft's rendition. It encourages one to consider Boudica's human side, offering a chance to explore more of the emotional aspects at work here than just the need for revenge.

Another frequently raised question about the queen is that relating to her actual name. In more recent times, the greatly popular version Boadicea was the name most commonly used when referring to the Icenian queen. As with her physical image, history has seen her name changed from its original version into several others which still remain as a source of debate to this day. The truth of the matter is that the original manuscripts of Tacitus containing the earliest known references to the queen were originally hand copied and, inevitably, misspellings occurred which gave rise to the different versions that we know of today.

Boudica, Boudicca, Bonduca, Boadicea and Buduica have all been put forward as the true name of the queen, but it is only the first version which should be regarded as the historically correct one. This particular version was first correctly applied by Tacitus and, in this form, translates as 'victory' in her native British tongue. The last version is the name which Dio applies incorrectly; and the most popular modern version, Boadicea, first appeared in the records around the seventeenth century, roundly demonstrating that, even after the relatively short passage of time between the accounts of Tacitus and Dio, enough transcription errors had occurred to completely obscure the true spelling of the name.

While we will never know for sure whether Dio got it anywhere near right when he described Boudica as tall with tawny hair and a harsh voice, we can at least satisfy ourselves that his description of what she wore has a decent ring of truth to it. Certainly, the mention of her hair falling to her hips fits well with what we know about hairstyles as worn by high-born Celtic women. As a noble woman, Boudica would almost certainly have grown her hair long and taken great pains to keep it well groomed. For such women, long, well-kept hair was an obvious indication of high status in the Celtic world given that only the most privileged would have the free time necessary to lavish so much attention on personal grooming.

We can be happy too that her clothing is also reasonably well described, with mention being made of her wearing a 'tunic of divers colours'. This description very likely refers to the wide range of checks and patterns, some similar to today's tartans, that were available in Celtic Britain at the time. Again, the wearing of such richly coloured garments would be representative of an open display of wealth. The overall quality of the cloth combined with the colour varieties and pattern complexity would all attest to the wearer's ability to afford such high-quality fabric.

A further prominent and common feature of Celtic style and dress that Dio mentions is her large golden necklace. This perfectly describes the often splendidly crafted gold torques worn around the neck by the more well-to-do of the Celtic world. The wearing of neck bands and torques was common to all levels of Celtic society, with pieces being made from various materials such as lead, copper and bronze, but the conspicuous display of fabulous gold ornamentation is again an obvious indicator of wealth and power.

Today, no examples of such status and craftsmanship come close to rivalling the immense value and superior quality of the vast hoard of gold torques recovered between 1948 and 1991 on what was once Icenian tribal land at Snettisham, Norfolk. Much of this stunning and magnificent collection of ancient Celtic craftsmanship is now housed at the British museum and serves as an example of the vast wealth of the nobility in Iron Age Britain. The exact reason why these torques were deposited at the site has still not been fully established. If, as some suggest, some of the pieces were deposited as votive offerings and ritually placed in the ground in religious rites, it perhaps calls into question exactly how wealthy the owners of these pieces must have been in order to be able to afford to ritually dispose of items representing such tremendous value. Whatever the collection represents, it clearly indicates that the Iceni possessed a tremendous amount of wealth at the time of the Roman occupation in the first century AD.

Having now explored both the reality and the myth of the image of Boudica, relative to how our modern perceptions have evolved, we will now turn to the handful of facts that history itself actually provides us with. This will then help to establish a clear political picture of the queen herself, before she rose up and burned her name onto the pages of popular history.

Though there is no way we can say for sure how old Boudica was at the time of the revolt, we do know that she was a loyal wife to Prasutagus. She was also a devoted mother to at least two daughters and, for a while at least, she was willing to embrace the Roman occupiers as allies and stand by her husband while he willingly took on the role of lackey of the Roman state. Along with Prasutagus, she enjoyed all the benefits that came with being appointed as the sole client rulers of the Iceni lands and people.

The couple's position had been gained only through direct demonstrations of co-operation with Rome, serving not only their own ends but also the interests of an invading foreign power which fully intended to profit from its occupation, initially at the expense of the indigenous population. They willingly joined a list of tribal leaders who had sold out to Rome, either in an attempt to ensure their continued survival or, perhaps more distastefully, merely from the anticipation of reaping the many apparent benefits, fiscal and political, of an alliance with Rome. No doubt Prasutagus and Boudica would have reaped all of the benefits and securities that came with the job, willingly paying a tribute to Rome in furtherance of that arrangement. For a few years at least, peace and prosperity prevailed for the Iceni. As for Boudica herself, she enjoyed a comfortable life, and the prospect of rising in bloody rebellion, with responsibility for the massacre of around 80,000 people on her hands, was something she would not yet need to contemplate. In fact, it was only when Rome decided that it wanted the lion's share of the Icenian pie that the good life came crashing to an abrupt and violent end and the cosy arrangement with the Romans inevitably turned sour.

GAIUS SUETONIUS PAULINUS, GOVERNOR OF BRITANNIA

In late AD 58, Gaius Suetonius Paulinus became military governor of the province of Britannia. His predecessor, Quintus Veranius, had died in post, completing only one unremarkable year in office. After the death of Veranius, Paulinus had probably been specifically selected as governor in order to complete the assault on Wales and finally deliver the territory into the hands of Nero. During the previous office, Veranius had done little more than assail the Silures, the tribe native to South Wales, with a few tentative raids before death finally curtailed his operations. Whilst we will never know what fruits Veranius's governorship might have yielded had he been allowed to see his time through as governor, we do know that he aspired to greater things than he actually achieved. The result of his planned campaigns, he grandly claimed in his will, would have seen him deliver the whole province up to Nero had he had another two years to see the job through. Despite Veranius's grandiose claims, it would be his successor, Paulinus, who would prove to be the catalyst for the almost complete takeover of the troublesome province and almost single-handedly wipe out much of the opposition in the southern half of Britain by his violent and bloody response to the aftermath of the revolt. The need to punish and exact retribution on those involved in the revolt would prompt Paulinus to sweep vengefully through the province, slaughtering probably many thousands more people than those who were actually killed by the rebels under Boudica.

Paulinus was born to an influential family around the dawn of the new millennium in AD 1, during the reign of the first of the Roman Emperors, Augustus. By the time he had reached forty, in AD 41, Paulinus had begun to rise through the military and political ranks of Rome and had achieved the position of Praetor. He was then posted to Mauretania in North Africa where he subsequently distinguished himself fighting against the Moors who were then taken up in violently resisting the attempts of the occupying Roman forces to take full control of the province. This is the first notable mention of the start of a long and distinguished career for Paulinus in the Roman political and military arena.

Whilst we know very little about his early life, Paulinus, in order to qualify for the subsequent appointments to Praetor and Consul, would have begun his career in the same way as any other Roman aspiring to high public office. He would have started at the very bottom of the ladder of power, working his way up the *cursus honorum*, a nominal roll rather like a *Who's Who* of Rome's great and good which listed each public position available and its holder for each year.

For Paulinus to take the first step up from the bottom rung of this ladder he would have needed to complete a total of ten years' service, either as a junior officer in the Roman cavalry, or *eques* to give it its proper title, or again as a junior officer serving on the staff of a general. Having duly served his ten years Paulinus could move on to completing the next stage in progressing up the list, which would have then been dependent on nothing more than capitalising on the merit gained either from the personal reputation he had forged for himself or by virtue of his illustrious ancestors' reputations. This round of shameless self-promotion would then indicate to the power brokers of the Roman world whether or not he was made of the right stuff and was indeed the required calibre of individual to progress to a higher office.

Having now made the required impression, his next rung on the ladder would be to achieve direct election to one of the available posts of quaestor. Up to twelve of these posts were open every year, and they qualified the holder for direct membership of the Senate. Various types of quaestorship were available, but Paulinus would probably not have chosen one of the more politically based roles. Instead, given his subsequent military career, he would have probably have held a position on the staff of either a general or a provincial governor. Excellent experience and an invaluable grounding for the roles in high office that he held later in his life.

Upon reaching thirty-six years of age, Paulinus could then have stood for election to the office of Aedile. It is most doubtful whether this choice of career path would have held sufficient appeal to a man with motivations such as his, as the post was not a legal requirement of progress through the *cursus honorum* and was more suited to those who wished to pursue a more politically based career. It is therefore likely that Paulinus would have remained a staff officer until he finally achieved the rank of praetor. Paulinus obtained this appointment at a point just beyond the earliest permissible age of thirty-nine years. Having gained the position of praetor could be taken as a good indicator that the ambitious Paulinus's career was well on track.

Whilst serving in Mauretania, Paulinus was given the appointment of *legatus legionis*, supreme commander of Roman forces in the province and a close equivalent to a consular rank. Although his name does not appear in the lists of the early empire which name the two annual consuls appointed to oversee military and civil matters, his appointment to *legatus legionis* is probably the most likely reason why he is later shown as a consul serving for the second time. His subsequent election to the office of Military Consul was duly recorded on the official roll in AD 66. Both military and civil consuls have lists of propraetors and praetors associated with their roles.

It could be argued that it was the manner in which Paulinus conducted himself while on campaign in Mauretania that influenced his later appointment as governor of Britain. The experience he had gained on these campaigns would have stood him in extremely good stead when it came to dealing with the problems that Rome was experiencing as it attempted to exert full control over the belligerent Welsh tribes. During arduous and intense campaigning in the North African province, Paulinus ruthlessly crushed the opposing Moors and eventually forced them to withdraw, following them up into the great Atlas mountain range and tracking them down to their remote strongholds, where he re-engaged them and subsequently wiped out the last of the Moorish opposition to Roman rule. He became something of a celebrity in certain circles, being the first ever Roman to cross the Atlas Mountains, and later wrote an account of his exploits in the region, giving the first detailed description of the range itself. Pliny the Elder subsequently made use of Paulinus's account of the country when he gave a brief description of the topography, flora and fauna of the mountains and the land beyond in his then definitive work *Natural History*, which contains a wealth of wonderful and often surprising observations about the world that the Romans lived in.

It was military prowess such as this that prompted a comparison of Paulinus to one of his contemporaries, the great general Gnaeus Domitius Corbulo. By the time of the Boudican revolt,

Corbulo had amassed a wealth of combat experience in different conditions all over the empire. He had held the governorships of the provinces of Germania Inferior, Cappadocia and Galatia, and in AD 59 he had led an army into Armenia where he had famously destroyed the city of Artaxata and then taken another city, Tigranocerta. Tacitus's opinions of Paulinus's motivations become apparent in this passage from his *Annals*:

> The new imperial governor of Britain was Gaius Suetonius Paulinus, Corbulo's rival in military science, as in popular talk – which makes everybody compete – he was ambitious to achieve victories as glorious as the reconquest of Armenia.
>
> (Tacitus, *Annals* XIV)

It would be due then to his skill as an experienced commander, combined with his proven ability to wage war in varied terrains, including mountainous country, which would have made him the ideal choice as the new governor of Britain. Veranius had not lived to fulfil his grand ambition to secure the island, and a more progressive appointee was needed who displayed the necessary drive and the proven ability to burn a path right through Wales and take the war into the Welsh interior. Here he would finally take the opportunity of squashing the resistance posed by such troublesome Welsh tribes as the Deceangli, Ordovices, Demetae and Silures and then finally fight his way on to the sacred isle of Mona (Anglesey), where he would purge the province of the outlawed Druid ringleaders once and for all.

There was no better man for the job than Paulinus. He was without doubt an experienced commander who had now repeatedly proven his worth as a sound and steady military tactician, amply demonstrating an ability to plan and manage campaigns by performing a full appraisal of the unique features of every engagement and then devising a strategy to defeat the opposing forces. Paulinus was dogged in pursuing his goals, a man who would see the job through whatever the difficulties. He would stop at nothing to achieve the desired outcome, even if it meant fighting in and mastering extremely difficult and hitherto unknown terrain. He was driven by ambition, he was calculating, he was ruthless and he was exactly what the Romans needed to bring Britain to heel.

THE CELTIC WAY OF WAR

To those people less well versed in aspects of ancient culture, the most commonly prevailing perception of the Celtic warriors is one of wild and ferocious barbarians who made no civilised contribution to the ancient world. They were more of a wild and free-living people, almost as elemental as the gods they worshipped and existing beyond the realms of the more sophisticated world of the Romans. It persists as a largely stereotypical image that has its foundations in classical literature and, more recently, has been built on by the romantic notions of the Victorian era onwards. During the nineteenth century, many countries in Western Europe rediscovered their ancient roots and fell in love with the great historical figures associated with their ancestral native tribes. Eminent artists, with a pronounced flair for the dramatic, duly presented the people with their long-lost images, or at least how they perceived them to look, by rendering them in the form of heroically stylised and proportioned sculpture. The British sculptor Sir Thomas Thornycroft began work on his rendition of Boudica in the 1850s and, some time after the piece was finally completed, she was placed in her current location beside the Thames in 1902, finally taking her place alongside the other great figures of Western Europe's ancient past that had also enjoyed a renaissance in the Victorian era.

Around the same time, the French people had rediscovered their Gaulish chieftain Vercingetorix, who was duly immortalised in a great six-metre-tall copper statue. This powerful image was erected in 1865 and stands now, looking out over the countryside of the Côte d'Or, not far from the spot where he and his warriors were besieged and subsequently defeated in the massive hilltop fortress town of Alesia in 52 BC, and where his campaign against Gaius Julius Caesar finally came to a bitter end. Vercingetorix, having finally surrendered to Caesar, was taken prisoner by the victorious Romans and was publicly strangled in Rome years later as part of the ritualised festivities to celebrate the great Caesar's victories in Gaul.

Germany too had its ancient hero in the form of the proud figure of Arminius. Many centuries after his death he was given the modern name of Hermann by Martin Luther, a name which would eventually come to be used for his statue and the one by which he subsequently became more commonly known. Even the name Arminius was a Latinised version of his original native Cherusci name Armin. A Cheruscan noble, Arminius trained as an officer in the Roman army before turning against the Roman forces based in German territories. His giant statue, the Hermannsdenkmal, created by Ernst Von Bandel in 1875, rises high above the Teutoberger forest near Detmold, celebrating the triumph of a chieftain who was the architect of perhaps the most infamous defeat of the all-powerful Roman legions when he ambushed and slaughtered three legions and their attendant column in AD 9. When their inept commander Publius Quinctilius Varus obligingly led his unsuspecting men into Arminius's carefully laid trap, a blood bath occurred which sent lasting shockwaves throughout the Roman world. So greatly did the disaster disturb the Emperor Augustus, who subsequently lost all of the territory east of the Rhine, he was frequently to be found wandering his palace for a long time afterwards crying out 'Quinctilius Varus, give me back my legions!' A Roman search party eventually located the shattered remains of the three lost legions some years later and finally laid their comrades to rest, but the XVII, XVIII, and XIX legions were never reformed, their terrible fate being something the Romans perhaps preferred not to be reminded of.

The site of such a bitter defeat for the Romans was lost for nearly 2,000 years and has only recently been discovered by

Major Tony Clunn, a British army officer who was serving in Germany at the time. His discovery of a coin hoard was instrumental in placing the forgotten battlefield close to the modern site of Kalkriese near Osnabruck. The story of Arminius's victory in German folklore and history, however, has never been lost.

All three statues portray an entirely romanticised image of what nineteenth-century perceptions would wish these heroic figures to look like. Now that our knowledge and understanding has moved on, it has become readily apparent that these magnificent sculptures actually bear scant resemblance to the real historical figures that they are meant to reflect. In examining the image that Thorneycroft has presented to us of Boudica, one can only conclude that the overall image is very misleading and, in order to provide ourselves with a more honest and accurate representation of the queen's likely image, we must disregard almost every element of Thorneycroft's magnificent work. Out must go the elegant classical-style clothing with its apparently clingy fabric, more reminiscent of light Mediterranean patterns. The use of such a garment is clearly historically inaccurate and really only allows the sculptor to deliver a more appealing form of the female figure. Instead, these should be replaced by fuller, heavier native garments. As discussed above, her hair too, although likely to have been well groomed and possibly lightly ornamented in some manner, would not have been scraped up and tied so tightly in the style that is portrayed in the Thorneycroft sculpture.

The inaccuracy of the portrayal is further highlighted when one examines how the sculptor has dealt with the grand war chariot that she rides in. Of the heavy-bodied vehicle we see now, splendidly decorated, armed with wickedly scythed wheels, and drawn by two magnificent chargers, the only element of accuracy we can perhaps attribute to it is the fact that Celtic war chariots were indeed drawn by a pair of horses. The solid wheels seen on the sculpture need to be replaced by a much more traditional spoke construction, fitted with iron tyres. Similarly, the bulky, decorated body bears no resemblance to the lightweight and more skeletal construction of a real Celtic chariot. Had Thorneycroft's chariot taken to the battlefield it would have been a heavy lumbering platform, totally unable to move with any speed or manoeuvrability. The actual Celtic war chariot would have been constructed with a low-profile framework. Its body components would have been expertly crafted from timber, tightly bound together with hide strips. Decorative features would have been evident which displayed the wealth and status of the owner, such as cast bronze decorations and woodcarvings on the frame terminals, and harness yokes rendered in the familiar Celtic artistic style.

The next element of Thorneycroft's sculpture that would require modification is the two magnificent horses that have been provided to draw Boudica's chariot. The sleek and elegant animals that we see now should in fact be replaced by stocky Icenian ponies of around fourteen to fifteen hands, far removed from the racehorse-like thoroughbreds that currently occupy the yoke on the sculpture. Finally, to complete the transition from fantasy to history, the vicious blades attached to the wheels of the Thorneycroft chariot need to be disposed of, their existence now identified only as elements of romantic fancy.

If this artistic image of how the Celtic war chariot looked appears so heavily flawed, then so too is how people most commonly perceive the way in which these weapons were deployed in battle by the Celts. If blame is to be laid anywhere for the misconceptions some people hold about the use of the war chariot, it should sit squarely with the filmmakers of Hollywood. The movie industry has been largely responsible for the misconception that such chariots were driven headlong into the ranks of their enemies, smashing a hole in defensive lines and then ploughing further into the formation, followed up by their accompanying infantry force, rushing in behind them to capitalise on the breech created. Whilst this portrayal of the use of the chariot in battle undoubtedly makes for riveting motion picture material, it bears little resemblance to the truth of how these vehicles actually operated on the battlefield.

The first commentary on their use by the Britons is given to us by Julius Caesar when he recorded the events of his first expedition to Britain in 55 BC. Caesar gives us an eyewitness account of the tactics used against the XII legion, which was out on a foraging mission when the Britons seized the opportunity of pressing home a surprise attack on the unsuspecting Roman Legionaries who, by this time, had lain down their arms and were busy harvesting corn. Caesar, having been alerted to the problem by his camp sentries who had initially spotted a large cloud of dust in the distance, quickly made his way towards his beleaguered men with reinforcements. What follows is his record of how the chariots were used against his men:

> In chariot fighting the Britons begin by driving all over the field hurling javelins, and generally the terror inspired by the horses and the noise of the wheels are sufficient to throw their opponents' ranks into disorder. Then, after making their way between the squadrons of their own cavalry, they jump down from the chariots and engage on foot. In the meantime, their charioteers retire a short distance from the battle and place the chariots in such a position that their masters, if hard pressed by numbers, have an easy means of retreat to their own lines.
>
> (Julius Caesar, *Gallic Wars* IV.33)

Caesar goes on to identify how the Britons' skilful use of the war chariot combines the best elements of cavalry and infantry power and credits their drivers with a high degree of control and manoeuvrability, even on poor ground. He also comments on the agility of the warriors that travelled on them, crediting them with the ability to run along the pole and stand on the yoke, and also to quickly remount the chariot when the need arose.

Caesar thus provides us with a brief but clear account of how the Britons used these chariots, and it is evident that he admired the great skill with which they were deployed. Moreover, his account demonstrates an extremely important element in how the

Celtic peoples made war. As is common with ancient armies, the advantages of displays of strength are clear. Huge numbers of men in ordered formations will often have a tremendous impact on how an opponent sees his chances as he closes with the opposing force and gains the opportunity to survey the enemy's strength for the first time. Morale can crumble in the most efficient of armies as they meet an opponent who is preceded by a formidable reputation or conveys a disciplined, efficient image, which will ultimately convey an impression of invincibility, further promoted by their sheer weight of numbers or the way they take to the field. Whilst it is fairly certain that a Celtic army would not enter on to the field in tight, rigid formations, the initial impression that their armies first made was equally important to the fighting ethos of the Celtic warrior. Conspicuous display was everything when it came to psyching out your enemy, and although their warlike efficiency would not have been demonstrated with a show of precision military science, the methods they did use still made many a classical army baulk at the thought of taking them on.

The Britons' use of chariots would have been a very unfamiliar way of fighting to Caesar's army as they raced round the battlefield. He clearly admires their ability as he describes their crews deftly displaying the skills he witnessed and the combined thunder of the hooves and wheels rolling round the field, deeply unnerving the assembled Roman troops who by this time would not know quite what to expect from these strange contraptions. Once they had got over the shock of this prelude to a full assault they would have recovered their discipline and prepared to repel the attacks, forming their ranks up ready to fight. It would be then that they witnessed the more familiar opening tactics that they had seen so many times during the years that many of them would have spent campaigning under Caesar's command in Gaul.

As the Britons attacked, their cavalry would be openly displaying the abilities so envied by the Romans who, lacking their own effective cavalry force, coveted the skills of Celtic equestrians.

The Romans so admired the skills of Gallic and Celtic horsemen, whom they recognised as among the finest to be found anywhere, that they wasted no time in recruiting them into the service of the army where they would become a key element of Roman military power in times to come.

The foremost element of the Celtic armies were the warrior champions, drawn from tribal nobility, who were the ones who displayed such great prowess in all styles of fighting, working from chariots, horse and on foot. Their training would have begun at a very early age, and their families would easily have been able to afford to invest the time and equipment needed to create a new member of the tribal warrior elite, as had their previous generations. Once these young warriors were fully trained, and had reached the age at which they were considered men, they would be able take on the traditional role of forming the nucleus of a tribal army. The physical training that they had completed would instil within them all the skills needed to proficiently wield weapons such as swords, spears and javelins, and would also nurture the code of behaviour that made them what they were, champions.

Being a Celtic warrior was not just about the ability to fight well. The role carried with it many aspects of culture and spiritualism that the initiate would also have to learn. These men were not at all like the production line soldiers produced by the Romans; as warriors it is clear they differed immensely. Whilst their weapon masters would have taught them the physical side of their craft, they would have learned of their ancient traditions and cultural identity from the Druidic brotherhood. The Druids carried out numerous roles in society, but one of those roles included the perpetuation of the history and culture of their race. A popular misconception exists that the Celts had no written language and were, by implication, uncivilised. The truth of the matter is that the Celts did make some use of the classical alphabets and also devised their own, called Ogam. Whilst evidence has been found of Celtic peoples using these to record day-to-day concerns such as grain harvests and stock audits, there is no evidence for their usage in recording Celtic history. The passing down of their heritage and culture was one of the reasons why a Druid had to train for over twenty years before becoming proficient in his calling. The Celtic people believed that their culture should be handed down in an oral tradition, believing that, if a deed or event had to be committed to actual record, then it was probably not worth remembering in the first place. Their past was sacred, and by being delivered in the spoken word, it was somehow kept alive. This then is the real reason why the ancient Celts have no written history.

The end result of all of this teaching would be a warrior imbued not only with the ability to fight but also with a strong sense of himself and where he came from – a spiritual being who operated along a ritualised code of conduct. He would be deeply proud of his skills and keen to demonstrate them to any and all comers. On the occasions when Roman observers had been in attendance at Celtic feasts and gatherings, they were astounded to witness such ritualised displays as engaging in single combat for the champion's portion, which was generally the thigh quarter of whatever animal was being roasted at the time. These contests were so fiercely fought over that a death was not uncommon, even if your opponent happened to be a blood relative! Whilst this sort of behaviour was deeply rooted in Celtic cultured it would only have served to justify the Roman conviction that these people were no more than uncivilised barbarians who were prepared to fight like animals over a piece of meat.

Everything about the warrior was about personal image. A formidable reputation was good, but to look the part was equally important. As well as open displays of wealth which came from the wearing of magnificent jewellery, finely wrought weapons were an equally impressive outward display of nobility and status. A finely crafted sword in an expensively decorated scabbard was the Celtic equivalent of owning a prestigious sports car such as a Porsche or Ferrari today. Fine cloaks with splendid brooches would complement the image and, at the time of the wars with Caesar, the warrior would wear either a mail shirt or just breeches. There are even frequent records of warriors going into battle naked. This was the ultimate display of courage and virility and, as well as a display of faith in the protection of his gods, it would represent the warrior's belief in an afterlife and his contempt of the fear of death. To complete his fierce visage he would possibly sport a large, walrus-style moustache, spike his hair with white lime paste, and cover his skin in symbolic or magical designs, either painted on with blue woad or tattooed permanently onto his skin.

Once on the battlefield, the warrior would make every effort to show himself off to the enemy, even offering single combat to an opposing champion. He would rhythmically beat his shield with his sword or spear and fill the air with war cries while, in the ranks of his army, war horns known as carnyx would blast out an eerie, frightening din, mixing with the clangour of the rest of the army as it sought to scare its enemy off the field.

Once battle was engaged, the champions would fight with incredible ferocity and took any opportunity to take the heads of their enemy, the more powerful the opponent the better. Severing an opponent's head from his body and claiming it as a trophy was an important practice to the warrior Celts as they considered the head to be the home of the immortal soul. To take a man's head was effectively to possess him forever. Heads were also greatly respected and believed to hold talisman-like powers of protection which could be used later when the head was taken home and preserved, to be revered and treasured and never to be parted with, even in exchange for great wealth.

Nevertheless, in the final analysis, all the effort put into showing an enemy what trouble it was getting into would only be really effective if such an army were to engage with an enemy which shared the same fighting ethos. The reality is that a Celtic army was little more than an untrained mob, drawn mainly from the farmers and peasants who worked the fields of their tribal homelands, and this is where the Celtic way of war failed so consistently when faced by Roman forces. The presence on the battlefield of a nucleus of fully trained warriors, even combined with exotic measures such as chariots, was frequently not enough to withstand the onslaught of a disciplined army like that used by the Romans.

The insular British Celts were at an even bigger disadvantage than their continental cousins when it came to dealing with the Romans. One could surmise that the British tribes of the mid-first century AD felt protected by their remoteness from the rest of the world, knowing that the Romans had tried twice already to get a foothold on the island and had failed. It must have been a widely held notion among the tribes adjoining the south and east coasts of Britain to think that the Romans did not have the required naval technology to land in sufficient strength to successfully invade, and that therefore they would content themselves with a continuance of the trade they had built up over the years. As for the tribes located further into the wild interior of Britain, Rome would have been a very distant threat indeed and not really worthy of concern.

If such were the prevailing attitudes among the tribes then there would be no reason to change. There would be no good reason to forge links with other tribes and form a confederation perhaps capable of defending against outside aggression. When one looks at the distribution of tribes across the British Isles, it should be with the understanding that no firm borders actually existed between the different territories and that possession of adjoining lands constantly swung back and forth as the tribes disputed ownership or attempted to expand their realms. If local negotiations failed to solve problems and quarrels, and Druidic priests could not settle a dispute by acting as intermediaries, then individuals, clans or tribes would go to war to settle the issue once and for all. This was how land changed hands, and this was the way it had continued for generations. The idea of universal accord amongst the tribes was therefore unthinkable. It would go against the very core of their Celtic cultural identity, contradicting the very order of their society and compromising their values. Other than the occasional alliance to further mutual aims, the idea of tribal unity was totally untenable.

It follows then, that on top of the implications posed by the traditional feudal society that was the Celt's world, there was also the added problem of the British leaders and nobles and their attitude to warfare. The tribal royals led from the front and the warrior champions with their client retainers were what made up their armies. These champions were men dedicated to securing personal valour and fame and therefore not best disposed to directing their skills towards building effective formations or working as part of a more cohesive unit. This mentality was present in both the chariot crews and cavalry and the higher echelons of the infantry. Its failure lay in the fact that its leaders could not effectively control and tactically direct a force of largely untrained peasants. Ultimately, it meant that the British tribes almost wholly lacked the ability to resist the onslaught of the Roman war machine in anything other than hit-and-run guerrilla tactics such as those successfully employed for many years by Caratacus.

The failing of a Celtic army against the Roman army was, generally speaking, the instability of the organisation which resulted from the existence of complex allegiances revolving around the clan loyalties and client system which was directly responsible for its formation. In single combat between champions, the outcome could ultimately see the victor of the duel responsible for winning an entire battle single-handedly. All forces could then withdraw from the field with honour satisfied and the dispute settled. The retainers of the warrior nobles faithfully observed the code that, whether their champion had won or lost, the matter was deemed to be concluded and no further bloodshed need take place.

Such rules of engagement were not readily observed by an opposing Roman force which, when challenged to single combat, would either initiate a full engagement regardless, or, on occasion, nominate a champion and allow such a contest to take place. It would not, however, be likely to withdraw from the field if the Roman nominee was defeated and simply launch an assault on the opposing Celtic force, possibly out of revenge, but more likely to complete the objective that winning the battle would ultimately achieve.

In addition to this, the ancient rules governing the Celtic force decreed that it was unlawful to desert your clan or noble on the field of battle. This could mean that, when facing a Roman army on its chosen ground, many men would be slaughtered on the field rather than yield, so long as the chieftain or group they supported remained on the field. Alternatively, if certain elements did take flight from the fray, it could mean that the resistance of a Celtic army could collapse almost instantly as clans, nobles and groups sharing allegiances fled the battle with their clients, consequently causing a rout to take place.

Perhaps the final irony of this analysis is the fact that this traditional and ritualised code of conduct employed by the native armies, for so long regarded by many as no more than savage barbarians, is something one would like to associate more with the so-called civilised Romans. Here was a military power capable of conducting brutally efficient slaughter, on occasion up to an almost genocidal level.

THE ROMAN IMPERIAL ARMY

It was the ancient Assyrians who first recognised the many apparent benefits to the state of maintaining a professional standing army. Since those early times, many different armies have come and gone but none has left such a legacy as that left by the army of Rome. Its organisational structure and adherence to strict discipline enabled it to complete staggering tasks and achievements which, even with the technology of today, some modern armies or organisations would find almost impossible to equal. As a fighting force the Roman army was truly formidable, but as well as having the ability to destroy, it was an organisation that could create too. The lands that were once part of the Roman Empire are today littered with testimony to the industrial and engineering brilliance of Rome's military forces. Structures such as aqueducts, roads and bathhouses remain long after their creators have gone, fitting monuments to the men who built them. Paradoxically, the ability of the legions to virtually terraform newly conquered lands and endow them with a wealth of beautiful, practical and enduring structures was equalled only by their ability to create a wasteland of destruction if required to do so, systematically killing every living creature to serve as a message to those who would dare resist.

When the army of Claudius came ashore in AD 43, the landscape and culture of Britain was automatically set to be changed radically and for all time. After landing in Kent, the Roman invasion force of around 40,000 men pushed inexorably inland and, one by one, most of the native tribes were brought to heel. After achieving the initial foothold in Britain, the Romans dealt with the business of installing all of the mechanisms of a new Roman province, dealing with the Britons using a carrot and stick policy. If tribal leaders were favourably inclined towards the invaders then they would reap the benefits of becoming a client state of Rome. The native King Cogidubnus of the Regni, now also referred to as Togidubnus, seems to have benefited extremely well from his own collaboration with his newfound allies, so much so that he decided to publicly and enthusiastically proclaim his profound admiration of the Roman way of life by endowing himself with the grand new name of Tiberius Claudius Cogidubnus. Although it is as yet unproven, he may possibly have further embraced his new pseudo-Patrician lifestyle by building for himself one of the most sumptuous classical-style palaces outside Rome itself, at Fishbourne in Sussex.

In truth though, while the Romans had their life made a little easier by the existence of certain other British kings who decided to choose clientage, they still had to subdue many of the native tribes in order to gain full control of their new acquisition. The early years of occupation saw much more stick used than carrot as the occupying army came down heavily on any native resistance. Initially, Caratacus was still free to cause problems and keep alive any ideas the natives had of ridding themselves of Roman occupation. A sweeping ban on the carrying of weapons by the Britons was imposed and vigorously enforced along with the imposition of the new military grain tax. To make matters worse, many of the native Britons were later thrown off their ancestral lands during the course of military operations to make way for such new innovations as roads and fortifications. Eventually, immigrant settlers intent on cashing in on the wealth of the new province thrived under the protection of the military, inevitably all at the expense of the locals.

As the ordinary folk of the native tribes, struggling to take all of this in, witnessed the embedding process begin, many would have realised that nothing like this brutally efficient power had ever been seen on the soil of Britain before. The Roman military machine was capable of performing many different and complex roles simultaneously, setting it worlds apart from anything that the Britons understood the functions of an army to be. Culturally the Romans bore no resemblance to the Britons and, as would soon become apparent, their treatment of the land and its natural resources would contrast totally with native practices. The army soon installed intensive industrial processes to rip resources from the heart of the earth, resources which had been taken by the Britons only on a much smaller and more environmentally friendly scale. The tribespeople around at the time of the invasion were seeing a military force at work which not only had the power to wipe out almost everything that opposed it but also rape the very land they lived on, occasionally leaving it contaminated beyond use even to this day. Though not known to either the Romans or the native Britons at the time, Britain would be a Roman province for nearly 400 years, and when they left the land would echo with Roman influence for many more years to come. The very notion of resistance would therefore prove pointless.

Despite the obvious negatives of Roman occupation, the echoes of that influence and the rich history of Roman Britain would never have been possible had it not been for the presence of the Roman army. The efforts of the legionaries in employing so many different creative skills steadily transformed the new province of Britannia, influencing not just the physical appearance of the place but the lifestyles and attitudes of its native population. This army could acquire a territory, provide it with a new urban and highly industrialised culture, transforming its old identity beyond recognition, and then, when the transformation was complete, provide the police presence to extend the order of the Pax Romana to the new province. Although alien at first, the Roman army's efforts eventually saw a new order established in Britain that represented a stronger, more stable society that had evolved way beyond its previous feudal culture. The economy was developing rapidly and a certain few of the increasing new elite were growing seriously rich. This was something which definitely would never have been possible without the groundwork laid by the Roman military.

It would not be unreasonable to say that the Roman army of this period was a complex and sophisticated organisation, comparatively not that far removed from the technologically advanced and logistically superior forces we can see in evidence in today's modern superpower armies. The ability to wage war effectively, then as now, is dependant on the discipline and training that an army receives. An army can possess some of the most modern and effective firepower but, without skilled and disciplined application, it cannot provide the true edge needed to win wars. In order to determine why the army of Rome was so successful then, we have to look at its cornerstone, the legionary.

If the Celtic warrior was all about personal image and the valorous deeds of the individual, his Roman counterpart on the other side of the battlefield could not have been more different. Here was a warrior who, just like today's soldier, needed first to pass certain basic criteria in order even to begin the gruelling training regime that would forge him into an elite infantry soldier. Once his citizenship had been verified he would need to produce a letter of introduction recommending him for selection. His height, fitness and former trade would all fall under scrutiny when determining whether he was made of the right stuff to become a legionary. If he passed this selection board, or *probatio*, he would then begin an induction programme based on strict discipline and the most gruelling of physical training. Here he would eventually be moulded into a professional soldier worthy of service in the legions.

His training would start with learning how to march at the designated military pace, building him up to meet the minimum requirement of completing a march of twenty Roman miles in five hours. He would endure intense physical training and steadily be introduced to progressively heavier loads to build strength and stamina, even learning to swim fast-moving waters whilst carrying his burdens. Mastery of weapons would be essential, from the throwing of a simple stone to wielding the infantry short sword, or *gladius*, to deadly effect. His skill at arms training began with using heavy drill weapons against timber posts, progressing on to going one-on-one against his comrades in sparring exercises. This training method, known as the *armatura*, also served as an examination of the recruit's growing abilities. Once proficiency had been obtained the soldier's skills were never allowed to slip, as the strict regime of basic training was reflected in his future service life with regular drills and exercises designed to maintain him at the peak of war readiness. This relentless round of daily training prompted the Jewish historian Flavius Josephus to remark:

> Every soldier is every day exercised, and that with great diligence, as if it were in time of war, which is the reason why they bear the fatigues of battle so easily.
>
> (Josephus, *The Jewish War* III.5)

Daily weapons drills were complemented by formation drills and regular monthly full-scale field exercises based on various deployment scenarios, perhaps acting in conjunction with artillery weapons or cavalry. Unlike the Celtic warriors, such intense and ongoing training would have fostered an intense team ethos within the legionaries that followed them from training to battle. This teamwork was ultimately the real key to the success of the Imperial Roman army.

If the legionaries were the bricks that Rome used to build its great army, then its centurions were the mortar that held it all together. These men were directly responsible for unit efficiency, discipline, and cohesion and they were not even averse to beating their men to the point of death if it meant that the lesson was learned. Tacitus gives us a clear picture of the brutal nature of such men in his *Annals of Imperial Rome* when he describes a centurion called Lucilius. A cruel man, he was nicknamed by his soldiers as *cedo alteram*, which translates as 'give me another' – a reference to his habit of striking the men under his command with his *vitis*, or vine staff, so hard that he would repeatedly break the staff and call for a replacement. It was not however beyond even disciplined troops such as the legionaries to snap, and this brutal centurion was murdered by his own men during a revolt in AD 14. Although Lucilius was probably the exception rather than the rule, it is easy to see how, under such conditions, unthinking killers were nurtured who slaughtered relentlessly on command, operating solely within the team environment of their units and adhering to a strict cult of discipline. These unit ties were further reinforced by the fact that no soldier below the rank of centurion was allowed to marry whilst in service. The only family they were officially allowed was their comrades.

Their home was the legion, around 5,300 men strong, and their career would last for twenty-five years if they lived that long. Despite its brutal culture it was for many an attractive career proposition, given that it offered clothing, shelter, food, regular pay and medical care, as well as many other fringe benefits including a savings and pension scheme and even a burial club. Soldiers served in groups of eight called contubernia, and ten of these made up a century of eighty men that was commanded by a centurion. It is generally believed that six centuries made up nine normal legion cohorts of 480 men with the exception of cohort one which was comprised of five double-strength centuries. Assorted support staff and around 200 mounted scouts and cavalry made up the rest of the force.

The legionary was also far better equipped than many of his enemies with a complete panoply of body and head armour, a shield, or *scutum*, and a variety of weapons for both close in fighting and for use as short-range missiles. Although a common minimum standard of kit and weapons was carried by the legionary, the overall appearance of a unit was by no means a uniform one. Different helmet types would be seen, along with differing patterns of body armour such as scale mail (*lorica squamata*), ring or chain mail (*lorica hamata*) and articulated plate armour (*lorica segmentata*). Although the legionary would have used a *gladius* as his primary weapon, this may well have differed widely in both its blade pattern and the types of scabbard used, from simpler forms to more elaborately decorated examples. The legionary's javelin or *pilum* too would have been of varying proportions and sizes, reflecting the differing patterns used in the various workshops where they were manufactured.

Everything the legionary needed to survive on campaign would be carried in his *impedimenta*, the Roman equivalent to today's large pack or bergen. This would have contained rations, spare clothing, bedding, eating utensils and entrenching equipment, all of which would have been carried on a *furca*, or carrying pole. Despite much debate and research into the subject over the years, doubt still remains as to whether legionaries wore a common uniform colour or whether various colours were employed, although off-whites and reds occur frequently in contemporary art works and archaeological finds.

Whilst the legions were elite fighting units made up of highly trained and motivated professionals, the Roman army also employed the cream of warriors from its conquered provinces as auxiliary soldiers. These men were by no means second-rate cannon fodder but often highly specialised troops in their own right. At the height of its territorial gains the Roman Empire was around 2¼ million square miles in size, a vast area embracing many different cultures and peoples who waged war in their own unique ways. Ever quick to exploit advantages, Rome used these specialist forces as *auxilia* to complement the legions. Levantine or Hamian archers were taken from what is now modern-day Syria, highly skilled bowmen who were trained in the use of the composite or recurve bow from a very early age. Formed into cohorts of 500, these archers were capable of deadly single-shot accuracy or a variety of withering volleys over varying distances. Slingers too were used from the Balearic Islands, as well as elite Gallic cavalry and the famous Batavian warriors from around the area of modern Holland who were capable of fording wide, deep expanses of water in full kit and emerging ready to fight.

Many of these auxiliary forces could be employed in various roles outside of full combat to conduct local actions and forays and complete peacekeeping or patrolling duties. The legionaries themselves used their vast array of skills in the building of infrastructure, forts and defence works and the enhancement of existing industrial and agricultural sites, their end products destined both for export to other parts of the empire and to feed the huge demand of the local Roman force.

It is small wonder then that few peoples were ever able to hold out for long against such a determined, complex and well-organised adversary as the Roman war machine. Disciplined and ruthless specialists who were dogged in achieving their goal, they would stop at nothing to complete the task, however difficult or daunting it might be.

2

CAUSES OF THE REVOLT

There is little doubt that a very large invasion force, even by the standards of today's military capability, was landed on the south-east coast of Britain in AD 43. Their progress was swift as they thrust inland, and in a very short time initial resistance had been soundly defeated. A triumphant Emperor Claudius made the journey from Rome and crossed the Channel, summoned by the invasion commander Aulus Plautius, to come and claim his first great victory. It is doubtful whether the bookish Claudius actually saw his invading troops engage the enemy, and far more likely that his presence at the final push of the opening phase was more associated with the symbolism of being present when the Britons finally capitulated. Surrender terms were subsequently secured from eleven British tribal leaders at Colchester (Camulodunum). Some of the tribal heads surrendered unconditionally, whilst others pragmatically embraced the arrival of the invaders, negotiating terms to become clients of the empire.

Antedios of the Iceni was one of the eleven British rulers present at these momentous proceedings and was one of those rulers subsequently granted client status by Claudius. His tribe had played no role in the Britons' efforts to resist the Roman invasion. This newly brokered arrangement with Claudius would now mean that, in return for timely payment of the usual tributes that they had agreed to, occupying Roman forces would not be garrisoned in force in Icenian lands and his people would be left to carry on with life pretty much as before. This arrangement would suit both parties as the Iceni could still enjoy a degree of autonomy and the Roman forces could continue to consolidate their hold on the new territory without having to drain resources on policing Iceni territory. Had the Romans not been so seemingly magnanimous in granting client status to certain of these leaders it would have been very difficult indeed for them to hold on to existing territorial gains, let alone carry out the rapid pushes further into Britain that they needed to increase their foothold.

Whilst no doubt distasteful to certain other British tribes, for the Iceni it was not an entirely unfamiliar arrangement with the Romans, given that they may actually have sought terms with Julius Caesar during his second incursion into Britain in 54 BC. This is suggested by a passage in Caesar's *Gallic Wars* when he recalls that, after engaging in numerous actions, he received deputations from several tribes who subsequently agreed terms with Caesar. Though approaching under a pretext of peace and goodwill, they were no doubt pursuing an ulterior motive of invoking his protection against the aggression of King Cassivellaunus of the Catuvellauni. Cassivellaunus had been appointed to head a tribal coalition formed in resistance against the Roman landings but he was also a threat to the interests of certain other British tribes. Therefore, by seeking terms with Caesar, the rulers concerned would be enlisting the help of a powerful ally. Caesar gives us this account of the occasion:

> When they saw that the Trinovantes had been protected against Cassivellaunus and spared any injury on the part of the Roman troops, several other tribes, the Cenimagni, Segontiaci, Ancalites, Bibroci and Cassi, sent embassies and surrendered.
>
> (Julius Caesar, *Gallic Wars* V.21)

The first of the tribes mentioned in this passage, the Cenimagni, are thought to be the tribe we know today as the Iceni. It is possible that Caesar received them as the 'Great Iceni' or '*Iceni Magni*', and that either the original text has since suffered corruption from subsequent rewriting or the name was misheard and incorrectly recorded when it was first written. Whatever the case, Caesar seems to be suggesting that, having seen that the Romans were perhaps a safer option than some of their neighbours, the tribes mentioned eventually arrived at the prudent decision to throw in their lot with him and benefit from the protection previously suggested.

If such was the case, and the tribe which Caesar referred to as the Cenimagni are indeed the Iceni, then the initial surrender terms which were negotiated may have subsequently led to the Iceni enjoying a much closer relationship with Rome in times to come. No doubt this was represented by the formation of trade agreements and diplomatic missions to strengthen their new links. If the Iceni had engaged in developing those relations with Rome, to such a point that the peace and prosperity that had resulted from their dealings with the Romans would be seriously threatened by joining native resistance against an invasion, then there would be no reason to resist Roman occupation and every reason to embrace it. After all, although the British tribes did enter into occasional alliances with their neighbours, their prime concern was for the good of their own tribe. It would not bother them overmuch if any of their neighbours lost out to Rome, as long as they continued to prosper.

The underlying problem that the Iceni ultimately faced from the arrangement was that of failing to fully consider the long-term implications of dealing with Rome. Becoming familiar with Rome did not mean that they necessarily knew all about how the Roman state worked, and at this stage the Iceni, as with the other British tribes seeking alliances with Rome, would still be operating under their own traditional conventions and expecting traditional outcomes. In seeking to serve only their own interests, they either must have been ignoring the lessons of the Gallic tribes or have been seriously naive if they believed that Rome would not later renege on the deal and take exactly what it wanted when it was in a stronger position to do so.

Some modern historians are now given to suggest that there was a Roman military presence in southern Britain long before AD 43, pointing to evidence such as Roman military equipment finds that predate the Claudian invasion. Whilst it would be unwise at this point to suggest, on the basis of such inconclusive evidence, that an earlier invasion date and venue is indicated by these finds, it could more sensibly be interpreted as evidence of military and diplomatic missions to promote Roman interests and strengthen alliances. It would not be unusual for visiting Roman diplomats and dignitaries to have their own small military force at their disposal whilst resident in foreign territories, and at this juncture the finds in question perhaps more comfortably support this suggestion than that of an earlier incursion in force by the Romans.

This argument gains more weight when the location of these finds turns out to be none other than the land of the Regni in Sussex, the kingdom of Cogidubnus. As previously mentioned, this client ruler was probably the greatest beneficiary of all when it came to becoming a quisling of the Romans. In assessing the many possible advantages of sweetening Cogidubnus up and gaining access to his lands, the Romans would have put considerable time, effort and money into getting him on side, perhaps even offering him limited military assistance which would have ended up being stationed in the area. Such a military presence would subsequently have left archaeological evidence of their occupation.

If, as suggested, Cogidubnus had been so carefully cultivated then there would be no reason to assume that this could not have happened with other British tribes with whom the Romans had been dealing, such as the Iceni. Although the Romans were able to land around 40,000 men during the invasion, any advantages gained by paving the way with the friendlier tribes would be a very prudent strategy towards ensuring the success of the invasion. The hinted presence of significant groups of Roman military and perhaps diplomatic personnel in a coastal tribal area, therefore, seems more comfortably to indicate not so much an invasion force, and more the activities of a politically sophisticated power laying the groundwork for an invasion by demonstrating and extolling the virtues of a Roman takeover, thereby sweetening the pill and gaining internal support for the undertaking of a large and risky venture.

Whilst consideration of the above points may offer a new perspective on these finds, the discovery of such finds in that particular context is of no more significance than seeing a modern jungle tribesman wearing designer trainers. Then as now, evidence for a more progressive society is to be readily found within the more primitive parts of the world without it actually being a significant indication of influence within that world.

THE FIRST ICENIAN REVOLT, AD 47

For the first few years of Roman rule in Britain the Iceni were able to enjoy, to a relative degree, all the benefits that came with being a client of Rome, along with the minimum of outside disruption to their lands. However, certain circumstances were about to prevail which would see the peace shattered in AD 47 as the Iceni took up arms against the imperial administration of the new province, control of which had then just passed to the then incoming Roman governor, Publius Ostorius Scapula. As the second governor of Britain, Scapula's time in office was a turbulent one which saw him forced to take a hard-line approach to the many problems he faced. Engaged as he was in repeated campaigns to subdue native opposition across the province, Scapula could not afford to display weakness or indecisiveness.

By the time of the first uprising, the Icenian hierarchy was becoming badly destabilised by internal power struggles concerning differing views on how best to manage their client status, and Antedios was struggling to stifle the growing resentment of certain factions within the Iceni to his pro-Roman style. Because Rome had appointed Antedios sole client ruler of the tribe he would no doubt have been happy to toe the Roman line in exchange for the stability and support that this would have offered him. Certain other influential parties within the nobility of the tribe, however, were not so enamoured of Antedios's apparent toadying to the Romans, and inevitably the factional nature of Celtic society took a hold and began to influence matters. Very soon Antedios was experiencing serious opposition to his governance and his position had become badly destabilised. The entire situation had become a powder keg just waiting for a spark.

The spark was duly provided later that year with the arrival of Scapula. The situation he inherited meant that he was unable to enjoy any settling-in period before having to take action to address the many problems relating to the control of the wild new province. Forced to act promptly, he decided to institute stringent measures to reduce any further problems with the hostile elements of the indigenous populace. One of his solutions would be to send in troops to disarm the native Britons in a number of tribal areas. It was decided, perhaps as a consequence of Antedios's ever-loosening grip on his own tribe, that the Iceni would be one of those tribal groups subjected to the new disarmament policy.

Although the decision to implement the policy may have been a quick decision made in haste, it is hard to understand why Scapula apparently failed to anticipate the consequences of the new restrictions. Not only were the Romans removing weapons from the possession of a client tribe, making a complete mockery of any local agreement, but they were also removing the ancient birthright of the nobility to display their wealth and status to their own people. Quite apart from the wholesale removal of all weapons in native hands, it would have been regarded as an intolerable insult to use common soldiers to openly strip the nobles of their rank as the troops ransacked their properties in the search of the now illegal weapons.

Their humiliation would now be regarded as complete in the eyes of their people. This was either a typical display of supreme Roman arrogance or an ample illustration of how little the culture and customs of the British tribes were understood by their new masters. Alternatively, Scapula may well have been fully aware of the likely response, and its implementation could have been carried out in anticipation of a violent outcome, a deliberate strategy on the part of Scapula to draw out the hidden opposition and thereby provide him with an opportunity to silence them for good. Whatever the reasons, the dissenting factions of the Iceni seized upon the opportunity to legitimise their now open disgust of Antedios's rule and rose up in armed revolt.

When hostilities finally did erupt the Roman forces moved swiftly to put down the revolt, and the uprising was soon squashed and over. The rebellious factions that had spent so much time sabre-rattling and stirring up the tribe were either dead or taken captive and doomed to execution. Somewhere in the melee, however, Antedios had lost his life, either killed in battle or murdered by those elements who so despised his pro-Roman stance. Ravaged by the battle against the Romans and leaderless, the future for the Iceni now hung in the balance as Rome decided what to do with them.

It was subsequently decided that another Icenian noble, Prasutagus, would be installed as the new client ruler of the tribe, and this is where his wife, Boudica, would begin her journey into legend as together they took their place at the head of the tribe. Having been installed as a client ruler, Prasutagus and his wife would now clearly be seen as willing supporters of their Roman masters. Perhaps they had even taken an open and active role in wiping out the opposition to Antedios and the Roman administration during the revolt. How else would Prasutagus have managed to secure this position if he and his immediate followers had not been so avidly pro-Roman? After such a potentially calamitous revolt, the imperial authorities must have considered occupying the territory fully in order to impose absolute control on the Iceni, who by now would have been smarting from the defeat and coming to the realisation that the loss of life had been to no avail. While resentments probably still simmered among the tribe, the Romans must have had great faith in Prasutagus to install him as their new appointee. Not only would Prasutagus have needed to convince the Romans of his unswerving loyalty, he would also have had to demonstrate sufficient strength and support to be able to control the tribe, even by threat of force if need be. At a time like this, a strong and loyal ruler would be crucial. Only then could Scapula relax a little and free up much-needed military resources for other tasks. There seems no other sensible reason as to why Prasutagus was allowed to succeed Antedios as client ruler.

Roman faith in their new man was effectively vindicated, as the tribe experienced almost thirteen years of relative stability under the rule of Prasutagus while all around them the world was changing and the Roman invaders were irreversibly establishing themselves. Scapula had died in AD 52, worn out by his efforts, but, to his credit, he had achieved the arrest of the rebel Caratacus and taken the fight to the fierce Welsh tribes who had suffered significantly as a result. His successors Aulus Didius Gallus and then Quintus Veranius continued the battle for supremacy against the Welsh tribes but failed to significantly improve on the progress made by their predecessor.

On the other side of the province the neighbours of the Iceni, the Trinovantes and Catuvellauni, were now paying the price for opposing the invasion. Fully subjected to Roman occupation, they could only watch as the old world they knew was slowly ground away as Rome exerted its influence and collected its dues. The Catuvellauni, under their king Cunobelinus, had originally seized Camulodunum from the Trinovantes around the turn of the new millennium, but by AD 43 the conquering Romans had seized the entire site and built the first ever legionary fortress in Britain on the old Trinovantean capital, or *civitas*, making it the garrison of the

XX Legion. By AD 44 a huge temple had been built in celebration of the victory of the deified Claudius, a monumental building which eventually came to stand as a huge alien-like symbol of everything the Britons hated about Roman occupation.

By AD 49 the army had long moved on as the XX Legion was needed to support the operations in Wales, but their veterans had established a great new settlement at the *oppidum* once known as Camulodunum, seat of the British war god Camulos. Now it was the site of the first Roman town, Colonia Claudia Victricensis, the colony of Claudius the victor.

First the army had controlled the area, then the veterans had ruled over the local Trinovantean population possibly even more inhumanely than the legionaries, driving them from their land and treating them no better than chattels as they made their presence felt and exacted all manner of harsh brutalities and humiliations on their defeated subjects. Had the new Roman settlers been more magnanimous and gracious in their victory, they may have been spared some of the cruel retribution that would follow. As it was, they continued to heap indignities and wrongs on their neighbours who, in their turn, simmered with building hatred and nursed an ever-growing thirst for vengeance.

In the winter of AD 59, the catalyst for one of the bloodiest chapters in British history finally came about when Prasutagus fell ill and died. Perhaps in an attempt to maintain a degree of peace and stability and to make provision for his family, the dying king had prepared a last will and testament which divided his kingdom equally between his two daughters and the Emperor Nero. If Prasutagus thought that such a will would help secure the future of his daughters and satisfy Rome then he was to be proved terribly wrong. Time would see all of his hopes come to nothing as, somewhat naively, Prasutagus had reckoned without the will of the Emperor and the monumental greed of his imperial agent, Catus Decianus.

DECIANUS ACTS, DISASTER LOOMS

Tacitus is brief and to the point in apportioning blame for the revolt when he recalls, 'it was his [Decianus's] rapacity that had driven the province to war'(*Annals*, XIV, 32). There are a number of apparent reasons as to why Decianus acted as he did when he moved in force into the territory of the Iceni, and implemented a shocking campaign of greed and blundering arrogance which would not only enrage the Iceni but also further inflame the resentments of their neighbours towards the Romans.

Cassius Dio indicates that Roman forces were sent in to act as debt collectors to retrieve money given to the 'foremost Britons' by Claudius. In addition, Dio tells us that the Roman writer and philosopher Seneca had loaned the Britons forty million Sesterces 'in the hope of receiving a good rate of interest'. This loan is apparently not one that the Britons either requested or particularly wanted but, nevertheless, Dio suggests that Seneca wanted it back in full. Being an extremely influential figure in Nero's court, Seneca himself would probably have had the means at his disposal to instruct the procurator, Decianus, to enforce its collection.

Tacitus, in setting down his version, lays the foundations for his later damning accusation concerning the greed of Decianus. He makes no mention of the debts owed by the tribes that Dio refers to and alludes only to the fact that Roman forces entered and plundered the territory after the death of Prasutagus. The following passage, underpinned as it is by Tacitus's accusation of greed, seems a more likely reason for Decianus's decision to subjugate and plunder the rich Iceni.

Prasutagus, king of the Iceni, after a life of long and renowned prosperity, had made the Emperor co-heir with his own two daughters. Prasutagus hoped by this submissiveness to preserve his kingdom and household from attack. However, it turned out otherwise. Kingdom and household were plundered like prizes of war, the one by Roman officers, the other by Roman slaves. As a beginning, his widow Boudica was flogged and their daughters raped. The Icenian chiefs were deprived of their hereditary estates as if the Romans had been given the whole country. The king's own relatives were treated like slaves.

(Tacitus, *Annals* XIV.31)

Perhaps there is an element present of the debt collection mentioned by Dio which goes some way to influencing Decianus's actions. However, given what Tacitus has to say, it seems much more likely that, far from acting in any legitimate official capacity, pure greed and opportunity were the overriding motives in Decianus's decision to enter the kingdom of the Iceni and systematically set about plundering its wealth and the possessions of its people.

As Imperial Procurator of the province, Decianus's position was unassailable and he enjoyed absolute power over the territories under his control. He could overturn any decree made by local magistrates and client rulers and he could act with almost total impunity in how he saw fit to govern the land and people under his control, even if his actions could be considered illegal or unjust. His position meant that he had the power to do pretty much what he liked without ever fearing prosecution. Many procurators saw their appointments as carte blanche for amassing great personal fortunes whilst in the post, illegally acquired or not. Decianus was no different, and he jumped at the opportunity as soon as it arose.

The procurator, upon learning of Prasutagus's death, would have moved swiftly to capitalise on the instability generated by the death of the king. It must have been something akin to a massive smash-and-grab raid as Decianus sent his enforcers in and the outrages began. Due to their apparently peaceful time under the clientage of Prasutagus, the Iceni may not have had either the means or will to effectively resist, choosing rather to formally protest at this blatant disregard for the will of the dead king and of the violated terms of their client status. What would have been perceived as gross impertinence towards the procurator and his agents would then have invited extreme and immediate consequences as Boudica protested against the injustices and argued the rights of her children and people.

Arrogance, greed, and crass ignorance would cause the Roman raiders to commit the gravest of errors as they dismissed Boudica's protests out of hand and decided to drive home the point by having her publicly lashed for daring to speak out against them. Then, further reinforcing the point that they were in sole charge and could do as they pleased, they raped the two young Iceni princesses who, by any standards of common decency and honour, should have been allowed to benefit from their late father's bequest.

Perhaps the Romans intended that the humiliations that they meted out to Boudica and her daughters would be taken as an entirely personal message, a taste of what could be expected if she continued to rock the boat. The real repercussions, however, would be much further reaching. Far from being a message to the surviving royal family alone, it served to outrage the entire tribe and amply illustrate exactly what the Romans were capable of. The very idea of nobility, let alone members of the royal household, being so outrageously defiled and humiliated, in public, by Roman slaves and common soldiery, was just too much to bear. This time the Romans had gone much too far. Soon they would be made to pay dearly for the privations they had heaped not only on the Iceni, but on their neighbours too.

3

THE FIRES START

THE TRIBES ON THE BRINK

A notable difference of opinion exists as to when exactly the tribal revolt took place. Was it AD 60 or AD 61? Alternatively, did the revolt actually span the two years in question? Although both years have been put forward many times in one version or another, it seems as though little argument has actually been offered to support the varying dates either way. In order to settle this issue we must look for clues in what classical records are still available for examination and add these facts to other variables that need to be considered in order to arrive at a satisfactory date.

The most obvious starting point is the death of Prasutagus, which, although not specifically recorded against any date in classical records, is largely believed to be in the winter of AD 59. Given the suggested dates that follow in this chapter, the second half of that year is the time which would correspond most closely with the information available. Once we are content that this date is correct we must assume that the incursions by the Imperial Procurator Decianus followed quite quickly on the heels of that event, as he capitalised on the instability caused by the power void left by the death of Prasutagus.

Many people believe that the revolt itself took place almost straight away after Decianus and his agents had plundered the kingdom and so cruelly violated the royal widow and her children. It is a popular assumption that Boudica and her tribe, unable to take any more of the abuse that the Romans were heaping on them, exploded into revolt and set off on a path that eventually led them to their fateful meeting with Paulinus sometime later in AD 60. Closer examination of the available information, however, seems to suggest that the revolt was not really the knee-jerk type of reaction that it is most popularly perceived to be. Certainly, one would be more inclined to believe that, unable to tolerate any more humiliation, the underdog rose up and finally gave the bully a richly deserved bloody nose, so to speak. Such a version is much more appealing to modern standards of fair play and righteous retribution. However, the popularity of this version has probably only served to obscure the true nature of the events themselves. Had the initial strike against the Romans been delivered in such a spontaneous and emotion-driven way it would most probably have been doomed to instant failure, as a lack of detailed planning would likely never have allowed the Iceni and their allies to achieve the victories they did against such a dangerous opponent.

If we accept that the revolt operated along a definite pre-planned strategy, we must first discard the possibility that it took an immediate hold in AD 60. If such were the case, then there would never have been enough time available in which to formulate such an ambitious plan to overthrow the Roman occupiers, besides which Boudica and her allies would have known that there would be no second chances. If they failed, the best they could hope for would be a quick death. A well-structured plan was therefore vital if they were to succeed in this most hazardous of ventures. The instigators of the rebellion would need to decide on sound military tactics to achieve their opening goals, they would secretly need to re-arm, and they would need to enlist vital support from neighbouring tribes, cashing in on the growing tide of resentment that had welled up against the Roman occupiers over the years. Boudica and her rebels would also have had an idea that the Romans would be expecting the possibility of a backlash and that they would be on their guard. Both Britons and Romans would still clearly remember the result of Scapula's disarmament policy and the lessons it taught. Allowing the situation to cool gradually would lull the Romans into a false sense of security, and when the time came to act their guard would be relaxed. The Britons would have only one attempt to try to seize their lands back from the Romans, and once they had started there would be absolutely no going back. Their planning needed to be exact.

The aftermath of the revolt revealed many things to the Romans, including the details of how it was planned and by whom. This is suggested in examination of our classical sources, and again it is Tacitus who provides evidence that the Britons had laid long-term plans in advance of the revolt when he provides a narrative for us on the thoughts of the Britons as they bemoan their lives under Roman rule:

> For ourselves, we have already taken the most difficult step: we have begun to plan. And in an enterprise like this there is more danger in being caught planning than taking the plunge.
>
> (Tacitus, *Agricola* 15)

Tacitus's reference to being caught further suggests that the planning was ongoing over a prolonged period. It is also worthy of note, in respect of further references to a date, that Tacitus mentions in the previous chapter of the *Agricola* that the governor, Paulinus, had enjoyed two successful years in office, the year of his appointment being AD 58. It could thus be argued that the specific reference to this plotting is datable to AD 60, with mention of the start of hostilities occurring later in the chapter.

Cassius Dio gives us further evidence of a specific date in the *Roman Histories*, opening book LXII with his account of the revolt:

> While this sort of child's play was going on in Rome, a terrible disaster occurred in Britain.

He is referring back to the last chapter of book LXI in which he describes Nero's institution of the Neronia, a quadrennial games festival, and also to the building of the Gymnasium Neronis. The former took place in AD 60 while the latter was finally dedicated in AD 62. Whilst no specific date can be arrived at from this particular piece of information, it is Tacitus once more, our closest source, who conveniently fills the gap left by this bracket. Tacitus states specifically that the revolt itself took place during the consulships of Lucius Caesennius Paetus and Publius Petronius Turpilianus – which was in fact AD 61.

The information that both historians supply, combined with other historical records, indicate that events surrounding the revolt span the two years in question. It would not be unreasonable to suggest therefore that after many months of planning which the Britons commenced in AD 60, the actual revolt took place in AD 61.

Having identified a specific year, as well as an apparent date bracket, it now becomes entirely reasonable to suppose that Boudica and her neighbours would have had ample time to put together a detailed strategy to throw off the Roman yoke once and for all. Once again, it is Tacitus who suggests that the Britons had in fact carefully planned their rebellion, in the *Annals* this time, as he follows his description of Decianus's outrages with this passage:

> And the humiliated Iceni feared still worse, now that they had been reduced to provincial status. So they rebelled. With them rose the Trinobantes and others. Servitude had not broken them, and they had secretly plotted together to become free again.
>
> (Tacitus, *Annals* XIV.31)

Surreptitiously then, the Iceni would have communicated with their neighbours, biding their time until the moment was right to strike and all the time honing their strategy and rearming as best they could under the noses of the occupying Roman forces. The Catuvellauni and the Trinovantes too would be secretly preparing for a war where only outright victory would do and Boudica would be dispatching agents to gauge support with any native tribes she could trust. Those tribes lying south of the Thames would scarcely be worth an approach given that people like the Regni and Cantiaci had benefited greatly from the coming of the Romans and would most likely reject any proposal which threatened their new-found wealth and stability, and probably even betray the plans of the rebels to the Romans to boot. As if to underline to us the futility of trying to enlist support south of the Thames, Tacitus even makes direct mention of the loyalty of Cogidubnus of the Regni when he tells us:

> Certain domains were presented to king Cogidumnus, who maintained his unswerving loyalty right down to our own times – an example of the long established Roman custom of employing even kings to make others slaves.
>
> (Tacitus, *Agricola* 14)

Boudica would be much safer trying to form secret alliances with peoples such as the Coritani who peopled the area to her west. Known also as the Corieltauvi or Corieltauri, their tribal lands ranged over a wide area, extending from the central and east Midlands and continuing up to the lands of both the Brigantean confederation and the Parisi tribe whose combined territories stretched across much of the northern half of Britain.

Whilst much of the Coritani tribe was apparently acquiescent of Roman occupation, a powerful faction of the tribe had voted with its feet and moved north, out of the occupied territories, to avoid having to submit to Roman rule. If such a tribe could be encouraged to lend its weight to the gathering opposition then things would begin to look very bad for the Romans indeed. Boudica would have known that if she controlled the eastern tribes and those of the central and south Midlands then she could shatter the bulk of Roman forces that would be deployed against her. These Roman units were now engaged in operations on the Welsh campaign, and gaining support from the Coritani could mean that she could effectively squash the Roman force between the advance of her huge combined force and the wild tribes in Wales on whom Paulinus was now waging all-out war. If she could achieve this then the Romans would be shattered as an effective fighting force and the remaining garrisons could easily be picked off one by one. Then, at last, the land could be restored back to its rightful owners.

COLCHESTER — THE JEWEL IN THE ROMAN CONQUEROR'S CROWN

Originally created as the capital city of Roman Britain, Colchester had, even before the Romans came, been an important location in the history of the local British tribes. Formerly known as Camulodunum, which roughly translates as being seat of the British war god Camulos, it was originally the ancient tribal capital of the Trinovantes, and remained so until, as was often the case with the native tribes, war broke out and the settlement was taken and subsequently fell under the control of the Catuvellauni tribe. Their prince, Cunobelinus, better known as Shakespeare's Cymbeline, expelled the Trinovantean king, Dubnovellaunos, and took the *oppidum* for his own in AD 9. Now regarding it as his new power base, he ruled from there, first over the defeated Trinovantes and then later as king of the Catuvellauni after the death of his father, king Tasciovanus, the following year.

Now that Cunobelinus ruled over both tribes, they became a powerful confederation which was subsequently recognised by the Roman state and Camulodunum itself was duly acknowledged by the Romans as a legitimised seat of British power. This powerful new alliance of two major tribes, however, was not averse to threatening the territories of their neighbours and pursuing aggressive expansionist policies which would eventually attract the attention, not to mention the displeasure, of Rome. Ironically, it would also be two of Cunobelinus's sons, Caratacus and Togodumnus, who would, by their intense hatred and suspicion of all things Roman, have a further unwitting influence in provoking a not entirely unexpected reaction from the Romans which would ultimately bring about the Romanisation of Britain itself. Hostilities opened with the sending of the Claudian invasion force to Britain and then, having brought all this down on their own heads, both of the brothers then led their tribes as chief resistors of the invasion that they had, in ignorance, helped to bring about.

As Cunobelinus's eldest son, it was another prince, Adminius, who was given control over the territory of Cantium, now modern Kent, by his father. However, Adminius was later driven out by the aforementioned brothers who took deep exception to his pro-Roman ways. Disgruntled by his treatment at the hands of his brothers, Adminius then sought help from the only quarter he knew would be able to provide it and made his way to Rome to lobby the Emperor Caligula to help restore him to his rightful position.

As it turned out, it was not Caligula but his uncle the new Emperor Claudius who accomplished this, not only returning Adminius home but also repatriating another ousted former adversary of the Catuvellauni. This man was Verica, King of the Atrebates, who had also been compelled to call on Rome's intervention the year before the invasion. Compounding the weight of the representations made by these refugee royals, the Roman court had also received demands directly from Britain insisting on the immediate return of the traitorous pair. This was now just too much for Rome to tolerate. Not only had the situation in Britain been deteriorating rapidly, these tin-pot British despots now felt that they could issue direct demands on Rome herself. Feeling able now to justify an all-out invasion, the Romans took the initiative that they had so conveniently been provided with and landed their forces in Kent.

The landing itself was carried out with little or no actual opposition, as the Britons had earlier received word that the Roman soldiers had mutinied in Gaul and were refusing to cross the channel. Hearing this, the Britons made the somewhat premature decision to stand their men down and allow them to return to their homes. What they had not banked on was the ability of Claudius's secretary, Narcissus, to move quickly to address the disgruntled troops and resolve the matter so quickly to get the invasion back on course. The subsequent surprise appearance of the Roman fleet off British shores gave the Britons no time to mount a defence on the coast and they were forced to allow the Romans time to establish a beachhead and the opportunity to advance inland before taking action. The Roman invaders eventually engaged with the resistance forces hurriedly mustered by Togodumnus and Caratacus. Togodumnus was subsequently killed during the early battles with the advancing Roman forces. Later it would be Caratacus whose legendary resistance would see him holding out against the Roman advance until he was eventually betrayed by Queen Cartimandua of the Brigantes and then taken in chains to Rome in AD 51.

For a while it appeared as though Caratacus, and much of his close family who were also captive with him, seemed doomed to suffer the same fate as Vercingetorix, but Caratacus subsequently saved the day by playing one final ace. Taken before Claudius and probably due for immediate execution, Caratacus stood before the Emperor as a man who had carved a name for himself as a worthy and noble opponent. His name had spread far beyond that of his homeland and people had flocked to Rome just to see this legendary rebel king. Caratacus did not disappoint and delivered a speech worthy of the most eloquent of Rome's public speakers, never mind a supposedly uncultured northern Barbarian:

> Had my lineage and rank been accompanied by only moderate success, I should have come to this city as friend rather than prisoner, and you would not have disdained to ally yourself peacefully with one so nobly born, the ruler of so many nations. As it is, humiliation is my lot, glory yours. I had horses, men, arms, wealth. Are you

surprised I am sorry to lose them? If you want to rule the world, does it follow that everyone else welcomes enslavement? If I had surrendered without a blow before being brought before you, neither my downfall nor your triumph would have become famous. If you execute me, they will be forgotten. Spare me, and I shall be an everlasting token of your mercy!

(Tacitus, *Annals* XII.36)

Of course, we cannot be confident that these were the actual words used by Caratacus, but we can certainly assume that whatever he said had a profound influence on Claudius. Moved to mercy by the impassioned speech, the Emperor granted Caratacus his freedom and allowed him and his family to live out the rest of their days peacefully in Rome.

Eight years before this momentous event it was Colchester, Caratacus's family power base, which was the scene of the collapse of further united resistance to occupation as it became the venue for the surrender of eleven British tribal leaders to the victorious Emperor Claudius. And so Colchester began to make its transition from a centre of immense tribal power and spiritual home of British resistance to a showcase of Roman imperial dominance, a perceived symbolism that would cost its residents dear in times to come.

The Romans quickly set about the deliberate obliteration of the old tribal seat, systematically blotting out evidence of its former significance. First of all, shortly after their arrival in AD 43, they built a fortress on the site to house the XX Legion. This had the distinction of being the first permanent legionary fortress to be built in the new province and its presence would have no doubt made an immensely powerful statement to the local population about the might of the occupying army that now fully controlled their former kingdom. As was the way with large Roman garrisons, the fortress attracted settlers to the new land who came from all over the empire, pioneering opportunists who sought to make a profit in the new province whilst sheltering under the protective umbrella extended by the presence of the garrison.

Within a year the civilian settlement had grown to a sizeable colony and Claudius, after much badgering from his retainers, had granted permission for a great temple to be built in his honour within the confines of the new settlement. Far from being just a mere place of worship for the army and the growing Romanised civilian population, this huge structure was yet another statement of Roman dominance. The native population would never have beheld anything like this immense shining edifice, towering over everything around it and looking for the entire world as though the gods themselves had taken a hand in its making. With its clean straight lines, enormous carved columns and magnificent friezes of polished, sculpted marble that adorned its looming portico, the natives would have seen it as totally alien and unnatural. They would have despised it as, every day, it looked down on them and reminded them of who was now in charge.

By AD 49, the operational frontiers of the Roman army in Britain had expanded much further across the country and the soldiers of the XX Legion had moved on to their new base in Gloucester. The frontier was pushing ever westwards and there was no sense in keeping a whole legion so far away from the new front lines. However, whilst the coldly efficient killing machine had moved on, it had left its own unique reminder of how brutal the soldiers could be. Now the old tribal capital was the home of the legion veterans who had recently retired and were eager to exploit the land and readily available sources of labour that surrounded their new colony. With a new name to complement its new Roman incarnation, Colonia Claudia Victricensis had swallowed the old Camulodunum up and now the brutal veteran soldiers were seizing the surrounding land and evicting or enslaving the Trinovantean population. As time passed the Trinovantes' resentment would have grown to an almost unbearable level while all the time the Romans, carrying on in their cruelly nonchalant manner, were effectively sealing their own fate, dangerously unaware that their supreme arrogance and cruelty was making them the architects of their own terrible and looming downfall.

FROM A SPARK TO A FLAME

With her strategy now in place and the backing of her closest allies secured, it was now time for Boudica to make a giant leap of faith. As confident as she might have been that her cause was a righteous one and that she had secured the support of her neighbours and her own people, she may well have wanted some final vindication of her plans. Just a little more evidence of support, this time from another, more divine quarter. In a world dominated by ritual and superstition, Boudica would not have made such an important and far-reaching decision without first seeking a favourable sign from the gods that the all-out revolt she was about to set in train was the only true course of action to be taken. In his account of the revolt, Cassius Dio describes a ritual which suggests how Boudica may have employed one possible means of receiving that much sought-after divine confirmation:

> When she had finished speaking, she employed a species of divination, letting a hare escape from the fold of her dress; and since it ran on what they considered the auspicious side, the whole multitude shouted with pleasure, and Buduica, raising her hand toward heaven, said: 'I thank thee, Andraste, and call upon thee as woman speaking to woman.'
>
> (Cassius Dio, *Roman Histories* LXII.6)

The ritual that Dio referred to was carried out specifically to solicit the blessing of Andraste, the Celtic goddess of victory, and it is interesting to note that Dio describes it as being performed openly, so that all of the assembled Britons would be allowed to bear witness that Boudica had received divine approval for the perilous campaign she was about to undertake. This apparent divine endorsement would no doubt have had a pronounced effect on certain persons present who, whilst openly enthusiastic of the plot, were still quietly wavering over whether to commit fully to the plan. To receive this endorsement from such an important and symbolically relevant goddess must therefore have been a potent motivator for the Britons, and one which would later require further tribute in the form of blood sacrifice in order to express their gratitude and devotion and maintain the favour of the goddess. This aspect becomes evident in the next chapter of Dio's account in which he graphically recounts how the captured Roman citizens were offered up as human sacrifices in the sacred Celtic groves, particularly those groves dedicated to Andate, apparently a highly revered goddess who, as the similarity of the name may imply, is understood to be the same goddess as the aforementioned Andraste.

Obtaining this divine endorsement for such a great undertaking was probably the final step in the planning stage, a small but important piece of ritual religious theatre meant to quicken the resolve of the tribes and finally galvanise them into taking the plunge and beginning the advance on the first of their objectives. Now that the talking was over the flight of the hare served to kick-start the Britons into action, underpinning their newly acquired faith in winning a great victory. But, if the planning had been much more thorough than perhaps first realised, it would follow that the actual start point would have been considered crucial to the success of the plan too.

Boudica and her allies would have wanted to begin the revolt at the most opportune time available to them, and there was never going to be a better time than when a sizeable part of the Roman army in Britain was engaged in operations directed against the Welsh tribes. In fact, by the time the revolt had begun, Paulinus and his assault force could not have been any further to the west, actively engaged as they were in destroying the last of the troublesome religious order of the Druids who had sought a safe haven on the sacred isle of Mona, or Anglesey as it is now known.

Today Anglesey is joined to the Welsh mainland by modern bridges, but at the time Paulinus and his force sought to make a crossing there were no bridges of any description to aid his passage. This fact, combined with the account of the end of the revolt given by Tacitus in his *Annals*, is valuable information in determining when the Boudican revolt may have begun.

As a highly skilled tactician and an experienced campaigner, Paulinus, having quickly made an assessment of the size of the problem he faced, would have taken up a position on the mainland facing Mona. Conspicuous in his presence, he would be letting his quarry know there was nowhere to go and that soon the Roman force that they could see on the opposite shore would be upon them. Whilst allowing the psychology of the Druids' situation to sink in, he would have made careful preparations to make an effective crossing en masse which, once achieved, would leave his troops instantly capable of engaging the fierce and determined opposition that awaited them the moment they set foot on the island. The Britons on the island knew that if the Romans were forced to come and get them it would mean death for everybody. With the prospect of such a fate at hand their only choice now was to go down fighting and take as many Romans with them as possible. For Paulinus's part, he knew how fiercely the Britons would resist, and knew too that half-drowned infantry and exhausted cavalry would struggle to subdue such a desperate enemy and that poor conditions would likely spell disaster for the entire operation. A bad crossing would therefore need to be avoided at all costs.

On Mona, he knew, there were many individuals that we would today regard as fanatics and terrorists. These people had fled, either from Roman-occupied territory, or in the wake of the advancing army as they moved towards the North Wales coast. There these outlaws would stay, like cornered rats, until Paulinus decided that the time was right to cross the Menai Strait and finish what he had set out to do. Mona at the time was, according to Tacitus, thickly populated and an area of great sacred and religious importance where ritualistic sacrifice was carried out, no doubt under the auspices of the Druids that he describes standing on the island's shore, cursing the army as they waited to cross. The governor would want to rid the province of the influence of this troublesome group of religious activists once and for all and he was now close to achieving that, although not at any price.

As a skilled and extremely tactically adept commander, Paulinus would not want to risk any unnecessary loss to his men. The men under his command were highly trained and experienced troops who were difficult to replace and his attitude to them would have been very far removed from more modern examples of leadership such as the careless, ill-considered assaults devised by the generals of the First World War. These were largely tactically inept senior officers who were a world apart from ancient commanders like Paulinus, as evidenced by the way they casually doomed thousands of men by sending them 'over the top', without ever giving a second thought to the resultant extreme carnage that befell their own men. In complete contrast to this, Paulinus would have identified the need to time his arrival in the area correctly in order to cut down the wait for safe crossing conditions. The onset of those more favourable conditions and temperatures would come with the arrival of spring.

The Menai Strait is some fourteen miles long and around two miles across at its widest point; it is tidal, opening out into the Irish Sea at both ends. Among its narrowest crossing points is where the current Menai Bridge spans the divide over a length of 710 feet. Paulinus would no doubt have preferred to use a narrow part of the strait to affect a crossing but the island's occupiers would have been very much aware of this and, demonstrating their continued resistance, they lined the opposite shore in a determined show of force, ready to repulse any landing attempt. Tacitus tells us that Paulinus achieved the crossing by the expedient of constructing flat-bottomed boats for his infantry whilst the cavalrymen either utilised available fording points or swam across the shallows next to their horses.

Even with favourable crossing conditions, achieving the landing on Mona would have been no mean feat for the Roman army that came ashore. Their general resorted to delivering a roistering speech in order to press the attack home. He needed to kick his men into action not so much because of the physical barriers of what they were being told to do but more the terror of the supernatural which, at first, is reported to have frozen them with dread as they faced the opposite shore and watched wild, black-clad women shrieking and brandishing torches. With them were the doomed Druids who raised their arms to heaven and drew down curse after curse upon the poised Roman force who, at first, probably believed that these frightening and mysterious priests held the power to bring evil on them all for violating their holy place.

Finally, hearing at last their general's entreaties, the soldiers snapped out of it and began the crossing with the infantry boarding their specially built boats while the cavalry swam or waded through the shallows, all of them psyching themselves up as they went and focusing now on the figures lining the opposite shore. Now that the dread spell was broken they urged each other on, convincing themselves that the Druids and their acolytes were now powerless to resist the fate that pressed down upon them.

For all their shrieking and cursing the Druids and their supporters on Mona must at some point have realised, as they watched the Romans drawing ever closer, that there was to be no divine intervention delivered this time. As the Romans approached the shore line perhaps some of the trapped Britons even questioned the strength of their faith as they heard the soldiers shouting out threats and insults, closing steadily in as though they were a great pack of baying hounds who had finally cornered their quarry. Thousands of soldiers were making the crossing, or preparing to, as Paulinus's entire battle group of the XIIII Gemina Legion and their accompanying auxiliary units struck out to finish the job. The waiting Britons must surely have realised that they had no chance.

As the Roman army hit the beach, vicious fighting would have instantly erupted as the Britons fought desperately in what they knew was a vain and pointless attempt to preserve not only their own lives but also the existence of one of their holiest sanctuaries. The screaming, shrieking women, half delirious now with a combination of burning rage and stark fear, would have set about the troops in a last act of defiance, only to be battered down by the crushing impact of the rapid advance as the soldiers hammered their shield bosses into their attackers and then finished them with savage thrusts from their deadly sharp swords, their mangled bodies falling under the feet of the relentlessly advancing formations as they pushed up the beach. As the Romans shoved their quarry further back into the island's interior, the shore line would have quietened somewhat as the clamour of battle left it behind and all the noise that remained was the ever-present breathing of the sea combined with the wailing and screaming of the wounded and dying. Broken by the Roman advance, they lay scattered amongst the corpses and the gore now thickly spread over the beach.

Further inland the main resistance would have been broken up into isolated pockets of Britons who, having initially survived the unstoppable surge of the Roman landing force, were now trapped on the island and had no way out. As the Roman forces fanned out over the island the small pockets of resistance would have been located, one by one, and either wiped out or placed in chains. The fortunate dead that now lay all over the island would not have to witness the savage execution of their revered Druids, watch children murdered and women viciously beaten and raped as the Roman army exacted the price of resistance. They would not feel the heat on their faces as the Romans sought out the places of abomination and they were forced to watch the sacred groves burn. Finally, their skin would not be torn and bruised by the rubbing of the heavy iron chains that meant that they shared the fate of the surviving few who were now the property of the Roman Empire. And so it was that Mona fell to the Romans.

The argument to support the spring of AD 61 as a start date for the uprising is further supported by more of Tacitus's writings as he later describes the cause of the resulting famine experienced by the rebellious natives with the onset of winter after the revolt finally collapses.

> But the enemy's worst affliction was famine. For they had neglected to sow their fields and brought everyone available into the army, intending to seize our supplies.
>
> (Tacitus, *Annals* XIV.38)

Certainly, this could be construed as further evidence of forward planning on the part of Boudica and her allies. It would maximise available human resources and have the added benefit of keeping the rebels fed without actually having to sow, tend and harvest their crops. It was, though, a very risky plan, given that there could be no guarantee of how much grain could actually be seized and also that it would be a time-sensitive tactic, in as much as the Roman forces that were regularly policing the tribes would eventually notice that crops such as emmer wheat, sown around winter and early spring, were absent from the fields. Once this absence had become evident, questions would be asked and the plan would be in serious trouble as the Romans would quickly begin to suspect something was afoot. If the Britons' strategy was to work, and the element of surprise was to be maintained, then the rebel force would have needed to move on Colchester by the early spring of AD 61 at the latest.

THE CLEANSING FIRE — COLCHESTER BURNS

In an act of the most astonishing complacency, the Roman town planners never saw fit to surround the original *colonia* of Colchester with any sort of defensive measures. It was only after the town was reconstructed, rising again from the devastation visited on it by the

Boudican forces, that it became a properly defended settlement with a surrounding bastion of permanent defences consisting of a high wall and deep ditch system.

In fact, if we are to believe Tacitus's account, it seems that the fate of Colchester and its unfortunate inhabitants could have been reduced in severity, even if its destruction was inevitable. His account of its demise begins with an eerie description of terrible portents, interpreted with dread by the town's population and later rewritten in an abbreviated form by Dio in the *Roman Histories*.

> At this juncture, for no visible reason, the statue of Victory at Camulodunum fell down – with its back turned as though it were fleeing the enemy. Delirious women chanted of destruction at hand. They cried that in the local senate-house outlandish yells had been heard; the theatre had echoed with shrieks; at the mouth of the Thames a phantom settlement had been seen in ruins. A blood red colour in the sea, too, and shapes like human corpses left by the ebb tide, were interpreted hopefully by the Britons – and with terror by the settlers.
>
> (Tacitus, *Annals* XIV.31)

Whilst this account of such dread portents perhaps carries little by way of significance for the modern reader, it was, for Tacitus's original readership, no doubt heavily laden with an indication of what was about to happen. The elements of disembodied shrieks, strange corpse-like shapes and bloody seas would have all served to set the scene as Tacitus made good use of literary devices, or *topoi*, to build depth and meaning into the account of Colchester's destruction. It has recently been suggested that the fall of the statue of Victory at Colchester is now not, as one may first have thought, a description of a coincidental occurrence from which a portentous meaning has been drawn. Instead, its inclusion is suggested to be the use of a *topos*.

In support of this suggestion is the fact that similar auspicious occurrences, directly referring to statues of Victory, are frequently related by Roman historians. One such usage is made, by Cassius Dio this time, in his introduction to the account of the Varus disaster of AD 9. Dio tells us that Augustus held the belief that, because of the sudden and catastrophic nature of the massacre, he must have incurred the wrath of a divinity. This was reinforced by portentous occurrences around the time of the disaster and, continuing the account, Dio then mentions that a statue of Victory that stood in the German provinces turned on its pedestal to face towards Italy, showing its back to the territory of the enemy. Clearly the similarity between the two accounts is evident as both statues are described as turning their back on the enemy as though fleeing. If this assertion is correct and the inclusion is actually a *topos*, then mention of the statue itself diminishes the value of the account in supporting the suggestion that such a cult actually existed in Colchester at the time of the revolt.

Other evidence in Tacitus's account indicates that, on top of the dire supernatural warnings that manifested themselves, there certainly existed enough physical warning of an imminent attack to prompt the town authorities to send to Decianus for help. Although impossible to say now, it would be very interesting to learn what Decianus thought of all this as he prepared to send aid to those people who were about to suffer the consequences of his actions. Whatever his thoughts, his woefully inadequate response was to send around 200 incompletely armed troops to bolster the small garrison that was currently stationed in the town. Perhaps he assumed that, with the existing garrison and his reinforcements joining forces with a town population made up of so many army veterans, that would be quite adequate to deal with the situation?

Boudica's plan for the destruction of Colchester was to work perfectly, as Tacitus implies that agents working within the town on behalf of the rebels sufficiently misled the defenders to the degree that they did not even prepare emergency ditch and rampart defences to counter the coming attack. In fact, rather than evacuate all those people who could not hold a sword, they chose to sit it out and send for the IX Hispana Legion for assistance. The web of deception that Boudica's agents had woven must have been a masterpiece of subterfuge to have been able to keep the entire population of the town in place as the tribal host fell upon them with an almost elemental ferocity.

Of the two historians who provide most information for us on this bloody chapter of history, it is Dio who provides the most flamboyant and sensationalistic accounts. His rendition of events is often a hyped-up version of Tacitus's work and he uses every opportunity to vilify and lampoon the Emperor of the time, Nero. Whilst this particular method of rendering the story makes one more inclined to suspect the validity of some of his work, Dio's horrific description of the brutality and cruelty to which the Britons subjected their captives is such that we are always inclined to want to believe that, in a somewhat macabre fashion, it may have a disturbing ring of truth to it.

> Those who were taken captive by the Britons were subjected to every known form of outrage. The worst and most bestial atrocity committed by their captors was the following. They hung up naked the noblest and most distinguished women and then cut off their breasts and sewed them to their mouths, in order to make the victims appear to be eating them; afterwards they impaled the women on sharp skewers run lengthwise through the entire body. All this they did to the accompaniment of sacrifices, banquets, and wanton behaviour, not only in all their other sacred places, but particularly in the grove of Andate. This was their name for Victory, and they regarded her with most exceptional reverence.
>
> (Cassius Dio, *Roman Histories* LXII.7)

In contrast, Tacitus provides us with a more restrained description of the killing, containing a reference to the price the rebels would later have to pay:

For the British did not take or sell prisoners, or practice other wartime exchanges. They could not wait to cut throats, hang, burn and crucify – as though avenging, in advance, the retribution that was on its way.

(Tacitus, *Annals* XIV.33)

Whatever the truth of it, there is no doubt that Colchester suffered a horrific fate. Devastated by the pitiless rebels as they killed, sacked and burned, the colony was reduced to a charred pile of ash that still lies in a thick band under the modern city, silently testifying to the intensity of the cleansing fire that wiped a town full of cruel and arrogant colonists completely off the map.

Just as the Romans had buried the old *oppidum* of Camulodunum, first under its fortress and then under the new town, so the avenging Britons had turned the tables. The symbolism would not have been lost on the rebels, particularly the local Trinovantes who had found themselves oppressed for so long by these brutal newcomers. Their sense of liberation and satisfaction must have been overwhelming as, after two days besieging the remaining settlers now holed up in that infamous symbol of imperial Rome, they heard the last screams of the doomed Roman colonists rising above the roar of the flames as the great temple of Claudius the Victor became their funeral pyre and burned to the ground around them.

LEGIO IX HISPANA, THE LOST LEGION?

The complete lack of defensive measures surrounding the *colonia* is an indication that the Romans thought it inconceivable that Colchester could ever fall victim to such a sustained and devastating assault as that which befell the town. It is not hard to imagine, then, the sense of complete horror with which the Roman administration must have been overcome when they later received the gravest word. In a shocking further development, added to the news of the town's destruction, a large force of experienced legionaries, sent to relieve the settlers, had been ambushed on their way to intercept the rebel force and almost entirely wiped out. The infantry force had been devastated, and their legate had only just managed to flee with his life along with his surviving cavalry force.

Much has been said of the part the IX Hispana Legion played in the story of the revolt, and accounts differ regarding where they originally marched from, where they met with such a crushing defeat and how much of the fighting strength of the IX was destroyed in that ambush. Only by examining the actual capabilities of the legion and the practicalities involved in moving such a force to engage the rebels will one be able to determine the most likely set of conclusions for this stage of the revolt.

The legion itself gained its 'Hispana' title from its time spent posted to the province of Hispania between 30 and 19 BC. Having completed its posting, it then served in Germany until around AD 9 when it was stationed in the province of Pannonia where, apart from one or two brief expeditions to the African provinces, it remained on active service until AD 43. The legion then marched to Portus Itius, now Boulogne in France, which was the assembly point for the Claudian invasion force bound for Britain. Once ashore with the original invasion force, the legion stayed on in Britain and remained on active service in the province right up to the time of the Boudican revolt and, around that period, was involved in operations which saw it located chiefly around Coritanian territories in the Cambridgeshire, Nottinghamshire, north Leicestershire and Lincolnshire area. Once the revolt took hold the IX Legion was the only heavy infantry force in the general area, and their legate, Quintus Petillius Cerialis, was presented with little choice but to act swiftly in an attempt to stop the revolt in its tracks.

At the time of the revolt itself, Cerialis's relief force could not, as some have suggested, realistically have marched from Lincoln in an effort to intercept the rebels. Despite theories to the contrary, there is no firm archaeological proof that, at the time in question, a garrison capable of holding a force of such numbers existed in the Lincoln area. At that time the legionary fortress of Lindum had not yet been constructed and that there seems to be no other evidence of any earlier military occupation capable of accommodating such strength in the area around Lincoln. The other, perhaps more relevant, factor to consider is that the actual distance over which the force would have had to march would have made successful interception from the Lincoln area pretty much impossible.

In determining where the IX Hispana set out from, deployment times are crucial. In order to present a credible argument for the location of the Roman base used and establish an overall timescale for this phase of the revolt we must look at the distances involved and the speed at which both Roman and rebel forces could move across country. Given that numerous surviving classical records provide us with the necessary data on how fast a Roman soldier usually covered the ground, this would seem to be the most appropriate place to start.

From his earliest basic training, the Roman legionary would have learnt the discipline of the regulation military pace and would have quickly developed the ability to cover the minimum required distance of twenty Roman miles per day's march. By comparison, the Roman mile is smaller than today's Imperial mile and in modern terms the Roman mile is expressed thus:

1 Roman mile = 0.92 Imperial miles, or 1.48 km.

In extreme circumstances legionaries could extend their march to cover twenty-five Roman miles per day, but this would prove to be a punishing distance even for experienced soldiers to sustain over a period of days, and certainly not one to be exceeded over a prolonged period if the commander wished to arrive with a force capable of immediate deployment.

By the time of the outbreak of the Boudican revolt, the Romans had constructed an established infrastructure in the occupied areas of the province and the pacified territories now had the benefit of a well-developed road system. With the advent of this network came an extremely efficient postal and courier system that facilitated communication so well that it would not be matched for speed until around the nineteenth century with the advent of steam power and the new rail network. Given the speed of the Roman messengers it would have taken little more than a day for Cerialis to be made aware of the revolt and to mobilise his force with the intention of intercepting and destroying the force of rebel Britons. If we assume that the rebel force could move at least as fast as a force of legionaries then we can begin to work out a probable scenario concerning how events could have unfolded.

Whilst it is by no means certain where Boudica set out from on her march to Colchester, it is most likely that she started out from one of two possible Icenian royal seats: either Caistor St Edmund (Venta Icenorum), often regarded as the Iceni capital, or Thetford. When a marching speed of twenty-five Roman miles per day is applied to the respective distances between these locations and Colchester, the approximate marching time for both is as follows:

Caistor St Edmund to Colchester: 62.8 Roman miles★ = approximately 2½ days' march at forced pace (25 Roman miles per day).
Thetford to Colchester: 47.5 Roman miles★ = approximately 2 days' march at forced pace.

(★The distances have been calculated from modern routes as a number of the original Roman routes likely to have been used no longer exist and cannot be reliably calculated. All distances are therefore approximate.)

Once Cerialis had received word of the outbreak of the revolt he would have had to move immediately, probably with the realisation that he might not be in time to save Colchester but making the assessment that he at least had a chance to intercept the rebels coming away from the stricken town. If he could achieve this, he would then be able to minimise the damage to other towns and settlements. In order to do this he would need the biggest force he could mobilise and one that was stationed close enough to the trouble to reach the rebel force in time. The garrison most likely to meet these criteria would be the IX Hispana battle group that was then based at the vexillation fortress just outside modern Peterborough at Longthorpe. This fortress was probably built around AD 48 as a direct response to the first Icenian revolt. It has been postulated that it was located at that point specifically to be able to monitor the activity on the tribal borders of the Iceni and Coritani and, in the event of problems, to deploy in strength as required. The fortress is known to have been fully operational at the time of the revolt, and would have accommodated a sufficient number of men, albeit not a full legion, to represent a very serious threat to rebel forces. Fortresses built to house entire legions normally cover around 50 acres (20 ha) of land but the site at Longthorpe covered 27.3 acres (10.9 ha). This still meant, however, that it was easily capable of accommodating over 2,500 men at any one time. Archaeological investigation of the fortress's internal buildings may even suggest that the IX Legion's first cohort was stationed at the base, which further implies that it was also the location of the most experienced and senior officers in the legion. Combined with ample evidence for a large cavalry force of around 1,000 (milliary), it could well be argued that the purpose of the garrison was indeed to act as a combined rapid reaction force, specifically stationed at that location to perform troubleshooting duties in the neighbouring tribal lands. At any rate, it would represent Cerialis's only real chance to react effectively and quickly to contain the revolt.

If we examine the distances from Lincoln and Longthorpe to Colchester then, even if a large garrison was posted in the area of Lincoln, it becomes starkly apparent as to which would be the most practical option:

Lincoln to Colchester: 163.24 Roman miles* = 6½ days' march at forced pace.

Longthorpe to Colchester: 102.5 Roman miles*= 4 days' march at forced pace.

(*Distances again calculated against modern routes.)

Boudica and her lieutenants would have had to take into consideration the existence of the Longthorpe garrison and, fully realising the danger that it posed, be anxious to remove it as a threat. She would therefore need to build her strategy around what likely action the garrison would take once they had received news of the start of the revolt. Given that siege warfare is notoriously time-consuming it would be tactically unwise to move to assault the fortress, either as one large group or by splitting her force and moving on separate objectives. At any rate, if the rebels made towards the fortress, Cerialis would have ample time to choose ground near to his base and wait for the rebels to come to a battlefield of his choosing. This would give him the opportunity to fight in formation and deploy the troops to their maximum effectiveness.

While the revolt was still in its early stages, there would be little confidence for a stand-up fight with a large, seasoned and disciplined Roman formation, so Boudica would need to defeat the Roman force by other means. If a set-piece battle was out of the question she would need to maximise her chances of victory by luring them to a place of her choosing and keeping the revolt flowing at a fast pace. To begin with though, keeping an eye on the Romans' movements would suffice.

It is reasonably safe to assume that both forces would have been regularly despatching scouts to keep abreast of the enemy's movements, and it is here that consideration must be given to how calculating Boudica's choice of tactics must have been. If she knew that the Romans would mobilise as soon as they had received word of the rebellion then she must have also realised that her only chance would be to destroy this first strike force as quickly as possible on her own terms. If she did not, she would be playing cat and mouse with a highly efficient and lethal enemy which would pursue her relentlessly until they eventually caught up with her and tried to crush her army on a ground of their choosing. The onus would therefore be on her to time her strike perfectly and eliminate the Roman force quickly and effectively if the revolt was going to continue.

Cerialis's force would have been moving swiftly along the Roman road system by now. Having left Longthorpe they would have marched to Water Newton (Durobrivae) and swung south on Ermine Street to Godmanchester (Durovigutum) and from there south-west to Cambridge (Duroliponte). The legionaries would then have passed close by their old base at Great Chesterford, Essex as they marched in a roughly easterly direction on a now lost section of the road system towards Colchester. It was probably somewhere between here and Colchester that the rebels fell on the unprepared column of legionaries and the massacre took place.

If looked at logically it seems quite unthinkable that the IX Hispana, their outriders constantly collecting intelligence as they moved towards the rebel force, just happened to march into the wrong place at the wrong time, just as a marauding army of rebels was leaving the ruins of the town it had so recently wiped off the map. It would be much more plausible to suggest that a carefully planned strategy was now falling into place as Boudica correctly predicted how the Romans would have to react. Their response would then provide her with the opportunity to wipe out the only force that had a chance of stopping the revolt from spreading. In the five days it would have taken to mobilise and march down from Longthorpe, the Boudican force would have had ample time to descend on Colchester, take the two days to reduce it to ash as Tacitus suggests, and then set an ambush for the approaching legionaries. The Britons could have misled Cerialis by allowing the Roman scouts to see a large presence still concentrated around the Colchester area and then permit them to ride back to Cerialis with the news while they hid a large force along the route and waited in ambush for the arrival of the unsuspecting legionaries.

It is tempting to think that Boudica may have learnt her lesson in countering Roman formations by hearing of the deeds of Arminius, the Germanic noble who so thoroughly wiped out three entire legions in a German forest in AD 9. In a catastrophic defeat for Rome, nearly 25,000 soldiers and assorted camp followers were massacred in a well-set trap sprung between a bog and a forest. This effectively meant that the beleaguered Romans could not break column and engage in formation-based tactics. The mechanical and brutally effective formation warfare that the Romans favoured was their tried and tested method of fighting that had seen so many enemies beaten. This time, however, there was no room for such tactics and, unable to adapt to the conditions at the time, the column was slaughtered almost to a man.

The march to Camulodunum would not have been easy for the troops of the IX Hispana as they pushed along the route at full stride, clad in full armour and carrying their weapons and heavy marching packs. Each night they would have stopped and pitched camp, sent out foraging parties and constructed a defensive ditch and low rampart around their tents that was complemented by the addition of sharpened wooden stakes to further frustrate any assaults on the camp. Sentries would be posted from the moment they arrived on site and rotated throughout the night until breaking camp in the morning and setting off again. Even the fittest soldiers would have been feeling the strain and fatigue of the urgent pace as they neared the end of the march and slogged along the road to Camulodunum, their forward scouts returning to tell their commander, Cerialis, that there was indeed still a large force of rebels around the devastated town. Many of the legionaries would have been battle-hardened troops, experienced at fighting a style of warfare that has been familiar to occupying troops for centuries. They would no doubt have relished the thought of slaughtering a bunch of hateful and unruly Britons and, professional killers as they were, the prospect of the coming battle would have made them dig deep for one last push as they closed on the rebels, ready to slaughter them.

For Cerialis, laying plans and devising possible battle strategies as he travelled along the route, anticipation of the coming battle must have turned to abject shock and horror as the rebel ambush descended on his unprepared and weary men. The jingling and clanking of their kit combined with the rhythmic crunch of their iron-studded boots on the road surface would have suddenly been lost in an explosion of noise. Chaos would have erupted as the Britons burst from cover and charged on them from each side, the ritual preamble of Celtic warfare now dispensed with by the Britons as they seized upon the element of surprise and denied the Romans any chance of gathering their wits. Their cavalry would have thundered in first, the riders screaming their war cries as they showered the column with javelins and then plunged into the formation, slicing with their long heavy swords and stabbing with stout spears. Warriors on foot would have charged in behind the horses, yelling their own battle cries and hammering their shields as they came rushing in. The Romans would have heard the unnerving din of chariots rumbling towards them and saw more javelins taking to the air as the charioteers reined in and deposited their warrior passengers onto the battlefield, these too seeming like screaming furies as they rushed the column.

No doubt the legionaries would have done their best to deploy any measures they could against the shock attack. Clamouring to form defensive formations and stumbling over the bodies of the fallen, the centurions would have vainly bawled out their orders, frantically wrestling to regain control of the column as the legionaries dumped their loads and made their weapons ready in the rising confusion. Relentlessly the Britons would have fallen on the column, their terrible ferocity charged by the murderous success that they had just achieved at Colchester. Any opportunity for the Romans to snatch a moment of respite to restore order in the ranks would have been denied them as each man in the column fought a desperate battle to survive. Cerialis would scarcely have believed his eyes as he watched his men being cut to pieces. He would have had to make a snap decision and, realising that the fight was totally lost, did the only thing he could to prevent the butchery of the entire column and instantly ordered a rapid retreat. In so well sprung a trap only the cavalry and other mounted personnel would have stood any chance of escape and, together with their commander, they would have turned back in the direction they had came and fled for their lives.

It is difficult to contemplate exactly what the legionaries must have felt when they saw their cavalry deserting them in a great cloud of dust as they stood their ground for the last time, with no choice left for them now but to die hard and honourably and go down fighting as the murderous mob hacked them to pieces. When it was all over, the victorious Britons would have shouted and cheered triumphantly over their ruined corpses. The rebellious Britons must have felt invincible as they pillaged the wreck of the shattered column, plundering the baggage train, stripping the bodies of the dead for weapons and booty, and hacking heads off here and there as gory trophies, suspending them proudly from horse bridles and chariots.

Boudica had timed it all perfectly. The Roman force had been caught completely off guard and annihilated. Crucially, she had not had to keep her force waiting for the arrival of the Romans for too long. If this had been the case then the force she had amassed may possibly have filtered away, satisfied now by the murder, looting and destruction they had just carried out. Their thirst for continuing with the revolt may well have been cooled by any significant period of inactivity and the momentum would then have been lost. This would have been disastrous, as it would have given the Romans precious time to return in force and wipe out everyone who had been involved in the uprising. Boudica needed to avoid this at all costs and it would be the astonishing destruction of Cerialis's column that kept the fire burning.

Now, not only was the capital of Roman Britain in smoking ruins but an army of professional soldiers had been all but destroyed, and all of this achieved in the space of a few days. This must surely have been interpreted as a sign that Andraste favoured the Britons and that the Romans' days in Britain were numbered.

As history tells us, much more was to come from the Britons, now taken up in the throes of all-out revolt. However, the fall of Colchester and the defeat of the IX Hispana represented a much greater significance than just the physical victory that was won at the time. By engaging and destroying the legionary column, Boudica had achieved her carefully planned goal and wiped out the only force in the vicinity that could oppose her. Now that it was gone, she had won valuable time to capitalise on her victory.

Perhaps more important still is an apparently overlooked but tactically important factor: it now also meant that she need not worry about the prospect of an attack from the east. By burning down Colchester, she would have known that any forces shipped over from the European mainland would learn that the town had been destroyed and would see little point in entering the Colne estuary and landing at Colchester's port.

Even before the Romans came, the settlement had been an important trading port on the River Colne, and this was a major contributing factor to the wealth and importance of the site. During the Roman occupation a large port complex controlled by the military was located around two miles from the main civilian settlement at Fingringhoe. Now the town had been utterly destroyed and all of the granaries and warehouses had been looted for supplies by the rebels. Any army landing there would have an immediate supply problem and would find it logistically impossible to quickly pursue the rebel force, quite aside from the fact that they would be placed in a situation where they would be forced to deal with the aftermath of the slaughter.

In the meantime, while Boudica pushed for London, Cerialis and his surviving troops beat a swift retreat back to the relative safety of Longthorpe. Some have suggested that his actions were rash and impetuous and consider his subsequent withdrawal to be somewhat dishonourable. Perhaps the real truth of it is that when faced with news of the revolt, he did what he deemed absolutely necessary, acting quickly in response to a very grave threat. Then, when finally he came upon the fateful encounter with the Britons, he saw that he had been duped into walking into a trap and identified his only option as a damage limitation exercise. He then took the difficult decision to withdraw, saving the lives of men who would have very obviously perished had they stayed and fought. Tacitus relates that Cerialis made his way back to the safety of his fort and subsequently makes no further mention of involvement in countering the rebellion.

Having survived, Cerialis and his complement of remaining legionaries, although apparently playing no further active role in the revolt, would perhaps later represent a significant component in Paulinus's strategy to beat Boudica. Given the garrison capacity at Longthorpe it would be safe to assume that, as previously mentioned, in excess of 2,500 men set off on that fateful expedition. This number represents only around half a legion's strength, indicating therefore that the other half of the IX Hispana were probably garrisoned in forts around the Midlands and East Coast counties in places such as Newton on Trent and Rossington Bridge. These garrisons were too far north to have ever have assisted in the early phase of the revolt, but still represented a sizeable force which could be mustered and moved south if required. As Tacitus recounts after the revolt is put down:

> The whole army was now united. Suetonius kept it under canvas to finish the war. The Emperor raised its numbers by transferring from Germany two thousand regular troops, which brought the ninth Legion to full strength, also eight auxiliary infantry cohorts and a thousand cavalry.
>
> (Tacitus, *Annals* XIV.38)

Clear evidence then that, despite Boudica's success in destroying half the legion, the other half was still available and therefore likely to be factored into any strategy Paulinus would formulate to deal with the worsening situation.

As for Cerialis, he no doubt resumed control of his remaining men and awaited instructions from the governor Paulinus. Clearly, had the Emperor and Senate later viewed his actions as incompetent and dishonourable then Cerialis would never have lived to go on to enjoy the high-profile career that he did after such an unfortunate episode.

4

THE FALL OF LONDINIUM

At this stage of the revolt it is easy to draw a comparison with two other key events in Roman history, perhaps the most noteworthy of these being the close similarity of Boudica's position to the situation in which Julius Caesar found himself in 49 BC. At this particular point in his career, Caesar, despite the success of his victorious campaign in Gaul, had ended up in a very difficult and dangerous position, given that the Senate had declared him an enemy of the state. In order for Caesar to extricate himself from this situation he was forced into making a very hard choice. Having carefully considered his options and with only a small army to support him, represented by the XIII Legion, he marched from the town of Ravenna until he reached a small bridge that would take him and his army over a minor river called the Rubicon. At this juncture, the choice he faced was simple: stay on that side of the river and remain an outlaw of the Senate, to be dealt with at a time and place of their choosing, or once more seize control of his own destiny and cross the river with the mind of 'so let it be'. Although a simple set of choices on the face of it, if the latter course of action were to be his chosen option then Caesar would be violating an ancient symbolic boundary, as the River Rubicon represented the limit beyond which no Roman general could lead his army. If Caesar did choose to lead his army over the river then this would be considered an act of high treason, an immediate military response from Rome could swiftly follow and civil war would erupt. After addressing his men and pointing out the dire consequences of this option to his troops Caesar finally made his choice and, throwing a hand in the air, Menander tells us that he cried '*alea iacta est!*' – the die is cast! With that he crossed the bridge with his army and yet another chapter in the pages of Rome's rich history was written.

Now Boudica was writing her own chapter in the Roman history books, and by razing Camulodunum to the ground and almost totally wiping out the IX Hispana battle group she had, in her own style, metaphorically cast her own die high in the air. In taking that first step on the road to all out rebellion she had put her trust in the gods and placed herself and her people into the hands of fate. Camulodunum had been her own personal Rubicon.

One further historical comparison of the Boudican revolt can be drawn regarding the way her army was subsequently swelled by its successes as she progressed through the province. Almost ninety years earlier and in a similar fashion, what started out as a small and desperate band of gladiators who had broken out from their school in Capua eventually swelled to an army which, although rag-tag and lacking in the professional discipline and training of the legions, became a force capable of threatening Rome's very existence. This uprising happened between 73 and 71 BC when the infamous Spartacus led his slave army on the rampage through the Italian countryside. In the same manner that Boudica's army would grow, Spartacus attracted thousands who, heartened by his successes, seized their chance to throw off the chains of servitude and make a new life for themselves. In typically arrogant fashion, thinking that an unruly mob of escaped slaves and criminals posed little serious threat, the Roman Senate initially dispatched a contingent of her

Urban cohorts to deal with the problem – a force that would prove to be totally unsuited to the task. The resultant shocking defeats suffered by the Roman forces only served to demonstrate to those living under the yoke of Roman oppression that hope did indeed exist. Consequently the ranks of Spartacus's slave army then swelled to even greater numbers. At the height of his successes, Spartacus was leading an army of around 120,000, and Rome came to fear that he might even be capable of turning up on its own doorstep and threatening the city itself. Heartened by those early successes, and fed by a steady flow of new followers, it would eventually take only the most enormous deployment of Roman military force to stop Spartacus and his army. Having come to terms with the fact that they had grossly underestimated the power of the slave revolt, Rome made arrangements to gather a massive force, and soon Spartacus was faced with the prospect of taking on a hugely superior Roman army.

Charged by the Senate with the job of stopping Spartacus, Marcus Licinius Crassus took command of ten legions and hunted the rebel army down. Eventually, and with the additional help of the entire armies of Pompey and Lucullus who had been urgently recalled to Italy, Crassus eventually managed to engage and defeat Spartacus and his army on a battlefield close to the River Siler in southern Italy. Fortunately for Rome, Spartacus's army, although proven to be a surprisingly effective fighting force, was poorly trained, lacking in proper military discipline and made up of certain disunited factions. It is interesting then to consider how the history of Rome may have been changed had these conflicting elements of Spartacus's army ever have found accord and decided to unite and launch an attack on Rome. A unity of purpose could well have spelt defeat for Rome, even with the protection of the huge force that was eventually mustered and sent against the slave army. As it was, the rebellion was crushed, and 6,000 surviving slaves were nailed to crosses all the way back to Rome along the Appian Way. Their brief cry for freedom from slavery and oppression was effectively stifled and it would be nearly 2,000 years before it was heard once more and finally acted upon.

The success that Boudica had achieved so far would have been seen in much the same way as that which spurred so many to flock behind the banner of Spartacus. It represented a great signal for those Britons who wavered on the peripheries of the revolt. Although many would have pledged themselves to the fight when the time first came for the Britons to act, still many more would have exercised understandable caution and held back to see which way events went, not yet committing themselves fully to the fight. Their heart would have been totally with the rebels but they would have been foolish indeed not to fear the terrible retribution which they knew the Romans were capable of exacting on them. Instead, they would have stood by at first and watched with eager anticipation to see if Boudica would actually survive her first big test or fail, being destroyed at the hands of a Roman army sent to put down the revolt. If she prevailed, she would have followers aplenty gladly flocking to her side. This uprising would not just be an opportunity for sack and murder; it would be seen as a ray of hope. Here was a chance to throw off the chains of Roman repression and go back to the old life that still existed in living memory, free of Roman imperial greed, brutality and interference. It would be this immense incentive which would eventually see Boudica leading a huge force, comparable perhaps to the army of the slave general Spartacus.

Whilst we cannot be entirely sure of how big the Boudican army eventually grew, it would not be unreasonable to estimate that it was at least around 100,000 strong by the time it met with Paulinus's force. Dio asserts that the rebel army initially numbered some 120,000, which, as his account progresses, eventually grows to an extremely unlikely 230,000. Tacitus on the other hand makes no mention of a figure, choosing instead to describe the number of rebels as 'unprecedented'. Unfortunately we will never know for sure whether Tacitus had taken the strength of Spartacus's army into consideration, so it is open to speculation as to whether or not he is indicating that the Boudican force was even bigger than the slave army. Perhaps a clue as to the capability of the Britons to muster a large force lies within Caesar's accounts of Britain as described in his *Gallic Wars*. Caesar states that the population of Britain is exceedingly large and that the ground is thickly studded with homesteads. It would therefore seem that if a large proportion of the population were inclined to unite and rise up, the potential existed to form into a very large body of people.

A further piece of information that may help to provide us with an indication of the strength of Boudica's force lies in the account of the casualty figures given in the classical accounts. Tacitus tells us that almost 80,000 Britons were killed in the final engagement against a Roman force of 10,000, with the Romans suffering only around 400 dead and an almost equal number wounded. It has often been said that these figures are the product of over-exaggeration to further enhance Paulinus's victory, but whilst it might seem unlikely that the Romans got off so lightly in the engagement, the figure quoted for the British losses may not be that far from the truth. As shall be examined in greater detail in later chapters, the way in which the Roman army was deployed at the final battle subsequently caused a rout of the Boudican force. This then caused them to run back onto their own baggage train and among non-combatants, allowing the advancing Roman force to butcher many of the Britons while they were hampered from fleeing the field. Whilst the opportunity to slaughter on such a vast scale is staggering to comprehend, it may not be the only reason why so many of the rebels died. Such apparent examples of mass panic have parallels in more recent history, in riots and football matches where the crush fatalities caused by a large body of people moving in panic have actually claimed more casualties than the perceived initial threat was capable of causing. Taking this factor into consideration, and adding it to the brutally efficient efforts of the Roman soldiers on the day, makes Tacitus's reported death toll of 80,000 somewhat more likely. As a result, this figure may assist us in feeling more comfortable with the earlier estimate that, eventually, the Britons outnumbered the Romans by around ten to one.

For now though, Boudica's opening gambit had paid off, and with the time to the next battle ticking inexorably away, urgent preparation was needed for the march on the rebel queen's next key objective, London.

PAULINUS IN LONDINIUM

Having received the initial reports of the uprising, Governor Paulinus would have been monitoring the situation very carefully as it was crucial for him to keep fully abreast of what had become a grave and rapidly worsening situation. With his subjugation of the isle of Anglesey complete, he could now afford to station a small occupation garrison to maintain control on the island. He could then quickly cross over to the Welsh mainland, taking the route east and embarking the XIIII Gemina Legion with their affiliated auxiliary infantry and cavalry along the same route, while he rode ahead in order to more quickly gather intelligence from the messengers as they carried it to him. Whilst it would be entirely pointless to speculate exactly when and where Paulinus would have heard of the destruction of the IX Hispana battle group, it is extremely likely that, having received such grim news, he would then have identified the need to make an urgent appraisal in person of just how dire the situation in the south-east quarter of the province had become. The size of the threat posed by the growing force was now crystal clear and he would need to formulate his strategy quickly if the Roman occupation of Britannia was to continue. The situation, he realised, really was becoming that serious.

The rapid flow of constantly updated intelligence reports would have informed Paulinus that the rebel army, having now utterly destroyed Camulodunum and beaten the IX Hispana, was moving away from the town and pushing south-west. Lying directly in the path of the advancing Boudican force were the nearby civilian centres of Kelvedon and Chelmsford, which, at the time of the revolt, had not yet developed into large population centres. However, evidence of a destruction layer datable to the revolt has been discovered in Chelmsford, amply attesting to the fact that, although the tiny settlement was of no great importance, it was not spared the attentions of the rebel force.

The lack of large centres of occupation within the general area therefore meant that there were no other targets of any notable size lying along the routes from Colchester to either St Albans or London that would attract the attentions of the Boudican force. In the path of the advancing rebels lay just a few military outposts of little importance and a small scattering of minor civilian occupation sites. News of the ongoing destruction of such sites being relayed to Paulinus would have further indicated the direction of travel of the Boudican force to him. This would allow him to reach the only possible conclusion that, because the rebel force was not reported to be travelling in the direction of St Albans, its next major target would have to be the developing commercial centre of Londinium.

Paulinus would have drawn a further benefit from the fact that, as archaeological evidence from places such as Chelmsford confirms, the Boudican army took every opportunity to plunder and destroy any targets in their path, no matter how small. This served to increase the marching time of the main rebel force and thus furnished Paulinus with an extended period of grace in which to reach London and make his assessment. Of course, the successful and wanton destruction of such soft targets would also further increase the desire of the rebels to carry on to a bigger and better target that offered an even greater opportunity to satisfy their growing urge to sack and destroy. That meant London was now effectively living on borrowed time.

Accompanied by an escort force of cavalry, Paulinus would have set off down Watling Street as quickly as he could, leaving the main body of his force to follow on behind while he rode directly for London to make a proper appraisal of the situation. The journey would not have been a comfortable one for Paulinus, as Tacitus hints at when he mentions him travelling through a land that was 'disaffected'. By now the news of the revolt would have spread far beyond the affected areas and reached the lands of the neighbouring tribes and beyond. Paulinus would no doubt have experienced the menace in the air as ordinary Britons began to receive news of Boudica's victories and, hoping deliverance was coming, openly displayed their hostility towards his party as they rode through the province towards the doomed town. This seething resentment evident in the local population would be yet another indicator to the governor that he would need to act quickly and effectively if he was to avoid the whole province rising up against Roman occupation. Time was a commodity he could ill afford to waste.

Upon arriving in London he would quickly need to decide if there was a chance to save the settlement and prevent the revolt from spreading further into the province, or whether the town would have to be left to its fate whilst Paulinus postponed his plans to engage the rebels until a more tactically opportune time.

Far from being the great Roman city that it later became, Londinium was at this time a new and relatively unimportant trading settlement that was home to a busy, reasonably sized port, centred on the busy commercial area of the modern city that is now called Cornhill. Its population was a cosmopolitan mix of local Britons, immigrant settlers and a varied cross-section of merchants and entrepreneurs from all over the empire, in fact almost like the population of today's capital in microcosm. Although not a greatly important settlement, it would have been quite a tempting target for plunder given the commercial activity that was carried on there and the wealth of some of its inhabitants. Like Camulodunum, the settlement was extremely vulnerable, having at this stage in its development no defence works in place to protect it. As for a military presence, the town was probably only watched over by a small auxiliary contingent that may have been garrisoned on the site of the old Claudian fort, a base that had originally been built around the time of the invasion to control the crossing of the Thames. This was a wooden bridge that had been constructed by the original invading legions as they crossed the great river and made the final push for Camulodunum.

When Paulinus eventually arrived in Londinium he would have immediately made a detailed tactical assessment of the settlement based on how well it could be defended given its location, size and available forces. Every aspect would have merited consideration, from the geographical location of the town and its natural defensive assets through to whether or not it would be practical and timely to summon reinforcements to defend the town. It would not have taken long for the governor to reach the conclusion that the situation was utterly hopeless and that there was no possibility of mounting an effective defence of the town. Paulinus would have known that the rebel army was closing fast on the town, perhaps no more than a day or so away, and the column ahead of which he had ridden would never be able to complete the march to the town in time to save it. Realising that the situation in Londinium was a lost cause, the best course of action for Paulinus would be to despatch messengers back up Watling Street, carrying orders to his force on the march to halt the column at a holding area and await further instructions. Paulinus had probably realised by this time that a head-on confrontation, at an imprecise location not of his choosing, would spell almost certain disaster. There would be no point marching the column further down into hostile territory until he had taken the time to formulate a sound plan to check the rebel advance. By this time, Paulinus was probably in no doubt of the fact that the force en route from Anglesey, combined with whatever other units he could gather in time, represented his only real hope of victory as he would only get one chance at stopping the rebel force. If he lost the next battle then the likelihood was that he would never be able to reform a force strong enough to re-engage the rebels in another battle. For now, it would make more sense for them to remain safely within the heavily militarised zone of the Midlands, close to the heart of the Roman road system.

However, Paulinus would have to cut his losses and leave Londinium to whatever fate had in store for it, turning his attentions instead to the urgent task of laying down his strategy for a battle that would need to be fought on his own terms. To make a stand at Londinium with the tiny force that he currently had at his disposal would be pointless and suicidal and would ultimately mean that the province would be totally leaderless. As military governor, Paulinus was now the only man with imperial authority left in the province, as the Imperial Procurator Decianus, having seen the catastrophic results of his clamouring greed, had quickly fled to Gaul. This left the problem firmly in the hands of Paulinus who, no doubt frustrated and angry that this catastrophe was not of his making, fully realised that he was on his own and would have to remedy the situation himself. (That said, it is difficult to imagine that Decianus, having been the architect of such disastrous consequences, would have been of any great use in trying to remedy the problem that the province now faced.)

Many of the inhabitants of the town would have been faced with a difficult choice once Paulinus had made his decision and given them the dreadful news that the town was to be abandoned to its fate. In the final analysis, the decision itself is not one that could ever be criticised given the options open to him, but at the time many of Londinium's citizens would have taken a very different view. Some of them had been there from the very beginning of the town; they would have been the original settlers who arrived soon after the military had established a garrison and then begun to build themselves a home and a future, starting a new life next to the river which would bring them their livelihood. Their pioneering spirit had laid the foundations for the new settlement, and many would no doubt have been mortified at having to turn their back on their homes and the life that they had made for themselves. Then there would be the merchants, many facing ruin because they would have to abandon almost everything they owned and run. There would be no time to gather large amounts of stock and transport it out as the rebel host was now almost upon them. Maybe the odd lucky ones had the chance to stow some of their goods on board those cargo ships that still remained tied up in port, hurriedly taking ship and sailing down the Thames away from the looming threat. For many others though, the only real choice would be to leave everything behind and run for their lives.

Some of course would have refused to accept the gravity of the threat and would have decided to remain, blindly convincing themselves that the rebel host would somehow miraculously pass the town by and that they and their homes would be spared the fate of Camulodunum. They would have taken the view that they could not turn their lives upside-down because of what people feared might happen, and that the expected fate was merely the result of over-exaggerated reports concerning the size of the threat. Feeling unwilling to give up their homes and livelihoods they would stay and sit it out, refusing to accept the awful truth of what was about to befall them.

Still others would have had no choice at all. The elderly, sick and infirm who could not be shipped or carted out of the town would have to remain behind and face whatever was coming their way. Denied a choice, they would be forced to wait for the rebel army to arrive. All the while they would be enduring the terrible dread and fear generated by the reports that carried the shocking news of the advance of the rebels. Wholly reliant on the charity of others, an unspeakable fate at the hands of Boudica's mob was something that they were totally powerless to prevent.

All of their choices made now, those who had elected to stay behind may have stood and watched their only form of protection walking out on them as Paulinus set off back up Watling Street, his small contingent bolstered now by a body of grim-faced troops which marched behind his cavalry. Once the Londinium garrison, now they would be more useful by withdrawing their protection, perhaps even to be used by Paulinus in the final confrontation. Their thoughts may well have been on what ever they held dear which they had been forced to leave behind. Whatever else they may have thought, it surely must have seemed as though they were deserting their town in its hour of need as the military governor led them north up Watling Street, riding at the head of a stream of newly homeless refugees, families and individuals who had grasped the real meaning of the threat that the rebel mob represented and wisely left while they still could, leaving the doomed town of Londinium behind. Just seizing the opportunity to stay alive had become far more important to them than the preservation of their wealth or possessions

LONDINIUM, A TOWN IN FLAMES

Nobody today can say for certain how long it took Boudica and her army to arrive in London after Paulinus and his column of soldiers and refugees had moved out. Perhaps the remaining population had as little as a day left before the town was finally overrun by the army of rebels and the burning and killing began. Those people who had buried their heads in the sand and stayed because they had dismissed the threat would have shared the same terrible fate as those who had, through no choice of their own, had to endure the crippling fear of what approached. Doomed now because, for one reason or another, they physically could not leave and were forced to remain behind with those stubborn folk who were now beginning to realise just how fatally flawed their decision to stay had been. It is quite an incongruous notion to think of those poor souls who were so desperate to cling to life but, because they were forced to stay, ended up with no choice but to perish with people who foolishly ignored the threat and decided to throw their own lives away.

As at Colchester, the archaeological evidence from London relating to the killing suggests it was brutal and indiscriminate. Women, children, the elderly and infirm were evidently all considered by the rebels to be just as legitimate a target as healthy able-bodied men when it came to slaughtering the remaining population. Even today, archaeologists make frequent grisly finds such as decapitated skulls representing both males and females of varying age and health. Those that remained were shown neither mercy nor pity. Nobody who stayed was spared the merciless fate that the rebels intended for them and, like Camulodunum; Londinium itself was doomed to burn until it was completely destroyed. It too would subsequently bear the awful scars of its fate by retaining a thick layer of charred debris that has remained below its more modern levels for almost two millennia. A layer that stands as stark testimony to the terrible fate that it shared with the first Roman provincial capital.

When one examines the overall importance of towns and cities throughout the Roman Empire, Londinium, unlike Camulodunum, ranked fairly low in significance and had yet to benefit from being regarded as anything other than an up-and-coming settlement. At the time of the revolt, as is suggested in the following extract from Tacitus's work, the town may not even have been recognised by Rome as a *municipium*. In other words, its citizens would not yet be in receipt of the rights and entitlements of citizens of an officially recognised Roman colony or town. Tacitus expands on this point by outlining what went on after the arrival of Paulinus, but never elaborates any further about the settlement itself.

> But Suetonius, undismayed, marched through disaffected territory to Londinium. This town did not rank as a Roman settlement, but was an important centre for businessmen and merchandise. At first, he hesitated whether to stand and fight there. Eventually, his numerical inferiority – and the price only too clearly paid by the divisional commander's rashness – decided him to sacrifice the single city of Londinium to save the province as a whole. Unmoved by lamentations

and appeals, Suetonius gave the signal for departure. The inhabitants were allowed to accompany him. But those who stayed because they were women or old, or attached to the place, were slaughtered by the enemy. Verulamium suffered the same fate.

(Tacitus, *Annals* XIV. 33)

Although dealt with in a later chapter, it is worth mentioning here that this passage is the only known classical reference to Verulamium, or St Albans, that is made in the context of the Boudican revolt. Cassius Dio does not even mention any of the towns by name, referring only to 'two Roman cities' as the targets of Boudica's attentions.

While Camulodunum would have had a much more established feel to it, Boudican London would have been more akin to a backwater frontier town. Although some evidence exists from early Roman London that indicates the presence of buildings made from more durable materials such as brick and stone, it would appear that structures of this kind were most certainly the exception and not the norm. London was only just beginning to evolve and it would be years before it achieved the true civic identity that prevails today after becoming the new Roman provincial capital, a foundation upon which the modern capital has seen its intervening incarnations grow progressively more strong and prosperous. The fledgling Londinium that Boudica put to the torch would have been almost entirely made up of timber-framed buildings, topped with thatched or wooden slat roofs, and enclosed by walls of wattle and daub. Even today the huge quantities of wattle and daub that were used in their construction are still evident. They are represented in the destruction layer as muddy brown or reddish smudges and sub-layers. These deposits graphically attest to the soaring temperatures that the fire reached as the heat of the inferno dramatically altered the composition of the material and subsequently changed its natural colour.

With such widespread usage of so many combustible materials employed in the construction of the town's buildings it would have taken very little time for the deliberately set fires to take hold and then accelerate to a point where the structures began to burn uncontrollably. Not, of course, that there would have been anyone available to attempt to halt the destruction, given that those who had not taken the opportunity to flee would, if not in fact already dead by then, be suffering the most dreadful of fates at the hands of the rampaging Boudican army.

DID LONDON HAVE TO BURN?

If Boudica had made the decision to ignore Londinium and march instead straight to Verulamium from Camulodunum, she may well have found herself profiting in the short term by effectively closing the distance between her own army and the force that Paulinus was going to confront her with. By using this alternative strategy she would almost certainly have reduced the lack of planning time available to Paulinus and may have pushed him into making an ill-considered decision that could ultimately have seen him lose the battle. Additionally, if Boudica was intent on uniting the tribes against the Roman occupation forces then it would have been much more advantageous to enter potentially friendly territory as quickly as possible and enlist their support. By destroying the Roman town that now occupied the former Catuvellaunian capital of Verulamium, the message that its deliverance would convey to the tribe would be a very powerful one indeed. They would see that the Romans had been unable to stand against the rebel force and were now finished in their lands. Under Boudica there was a chance to return to their old lives, free of Rome once more. Seduced by the idea of reclaiming their old lives, the Catuvellauni would have eagerly thrown in their lot with what they would have seen as an army of liberation, irresistibly sweeping through the land.

By examining the routes of today and their distances between the towns, it can be calculated that St Albans is only around five miles further from Colchester than London. As has been explored, travelling to Verulamium first would mean that Boudica would swell her ranks with the Catuvellauni quicker and be able to hasten the pace in her favour by taking the fight to the Romans earlier and forcing their hand. Even if the time taken to completely destroy Londinium is removed from the equation, by marching on that town she was still adding another day to her march to Verulamium by opting for the more circuitous route. In reality it would probably have taken a minimum of three days to complete the destruction of Londinium and then march to Verulamium. Boudica would have needed a very good reason indeed to extend her march from Camulodunum to Verulamium, raising the minimum marching time from three days to six days and thereby missing the opportunity to keep the Romans on the back foot. If Boudica's tactics were apparently running to a bigger plan, why did she make the decision to throw away such an opportunity?

It has previously been suggested that the area occupied by early London was actually within the territory of the Catuvellauni, but given the constantly shifting territorial borders of Celtic Britain, it would be hard to imagine how any one tribe would be able to lay conclusive claim to it, especially since it sits in an area where the territories of the Catuvellauni, the Regni and the Cantiaci converge. Given that, to our knowledge, nothing important previously existed there, such as a large tribal settlement or important sacred site, the rebels' subsequent reclamation by force of arms of such a piece of land would not in itself represent anything of any great tribal significance. Neither the Catuvellauni nor the Trinovantes would have had any great interest in the land itself, since the Romans apparently did not occupy anything of any real tribal significance when they first founded the town. Consequently, it seems very hard at first to begin to understand why Boudica, who has seemingly so far deployed such sound tactics, then wasted such a promising opportunity to force the unprepared Romans' hand by then deciding to plunder and sack Londinium, a town so disadvantageously far away from the next obvious target. Only in examining this early London a little more closely does it begin to become abundantly clear as to why it did represent a very strategically important target that would need to be swiftly dealt with before Boudica and her rebels could confidently move on to retake the old Catuvellaunian capital.

In geographical terms, the River Thames, on which London sits, represents the perfect natural boundary between the tribes living on each side of its expanse. As a major river, it is for the most part not easily traversable without the aid of a bridge or boat. Since its initial foundation London had been centred on the only major bridge crossing over the Thames after it was built by the Roman military during the opening campaigns of the invasion. This would make the seemingly unimportant town very strategically significant indeed. Further underpinning that importance is the fact that the bridge lies at a major convergence of the Roman road system. At the time of the revolt, this was the only location on the Thames where the Roman road crossed over, making the use of the bridge essential to anybody wishing to move quickly up and down the province.

If Boudica herself were to use this bridge to cross into southern Britain then she would be choosing to place herself into a situation that would be catastrophic to her cause. Not only would she be turning her back on Paulinus, but she would be marching into the lands of the distinctly more pro-Roman tribes of the Cantiaci and the Regni. If the rebels spread far enough west, they would touch on the lands of their neighbours the Atrebates who, like the Cantiaci, had suffered to one degree or another from the aggressive activities of their neighbours north of the Thames, years before the arrival of the Romans. The coming of the Roman invaders had finally put an end to the expansionist activities of the likes of the Catuvellauni and now, free from the threat of their old neighbours, the south-eastern tribes were prospering. They would have no desire to join the uprising and ultimately, if the revolt succeeded, return to the days of being threatened by their more powerful neighbours. They would no doubt choose instead to seize the opportunity to assist in putting the revolt down in any way they could, thereby securing further kudos with their new Roman masters.

By entering these tribal territories, therefore, Boudica would expose herself to attack from all sides and almost certainly suffer total annihilation. It thus becomes apparent that, given the tribes with whom Boudica had thrown in her lot, attempting to enlist the help of the southern British tribes did not represent a viable option to her.

What would encourage Boudica to march her force on Londinium would be the possibility that, if the bridge were to be left intact, she could find herself having to defend her rear while she marched on and engaged the forces of Paulinus. If, on the other hand, the bridge was destroyed it would then mean that any troops marching up from the south-eastern cantons would no longer be able to use the bridge to cross the Thames and mount a speedy pursuit of the rebels. If arduous, time-consuming cross-country marches and dangerous river fordings were to be avoided by Roman forces, any land-based troops in those southern areas would have to make for the town of Calleva Atrebatum, now Silchester. Here they would be able to pick up the nearest of the major roads and eventually end up travelling north on either Watling Street or, more unlikely due to the distance, joining the Fosse Way.

If the destruction of the bridge would thwart any chance for Roman relief forces to be deployed from the south of Britain, the total destruction of the town would also cause major problems with any attempt to sail a relief force up the Thames and land them at London. Successfully landing troops here would mean that they could join the road system straight away and rapidly move off in pursuit of the Boudican force. This would allow Paulinus to trap Boudica's rebels between his army and the pursuing relief force, thereby deploying a hammer-and-anvil-style tactic to wipe the rebel force out once and for all.

However, any force being landed to carry out such a task would need to be quite a sizable one, probably comprising a large infantry force and a cavalry contingent which might even need shipping over from Gaul, in the absence of a suitable garrison based on British soil. As with the previous situation at Camulodunum, the disembarking force would be met with a scene of utter devastation where nothing useful would have been left behind to provide them with any sort of advantage. Should the Romans choose to despatch such a force to join the road system at London, they would have to make provision for basic rations for the troops and for adequate supplies of fodder for the cavalry mounts and pack animals in their baggage train. Without these basic supplies the relief force would not be able to proceed any further. Even if they did decide to press on regardless, Boudica's army would be stripping available supplies for their own use as they went, no doubt making a point of destroying anything that would serve to further frustrate the progress of any Roman force bringing up their rear.

Of course, such a logistical problem would not pose any lasting difficulty to the resourceful Romans, but the key consideration would be how long their solutions to the problems would take to put in place. By the time the force had been assembled and the necessary stores had been gathered up to set up a supply base with which to maintain their advance, critical days would be lost and Boudica would have extended the gap between her and them, making it virtually impossible to catch up before it was all too late. This would also be the case if the Romans decided to try to rebuild the Thames crossing by setting up a temporary pontoon bridge. Although it would have been easy enough for Roman forces to carry out this task, it would require a unit capable of constructing such a bridge firstly to march to London and then to gather all of the components necessary to complete the bridge. Again, it would be time that would be the real enemy.

So far, most of the points raised above concerning the notion of how well Boudica's tactics actually worked seem to be no more than informed speculation. However, if that supposition is reinforced by the addition of recent archaeological evidence to support these theories, the calculating manner of the use of these tactics seems to become more readily apparent.

Between 1991 and 1998, the Museum of London carried out archaeological digs in conjunction with extension works to the Jubilee Line of the London Underground system. Prior to the advent of the evidence unearthed as a result of this work, it was largely believed that the area of Roman London attacked and destroyed by Boudica was located entirely on the northern side of the Thames. The subsequent archaeological excavations in fact reveal that a destruction layer datable to the time of the rebellion was also evident on the south bank of the Thames under what is now Southwark. Eventually a large area was cleared and explored which clearly indicated that a number of early Roman buildings had been totally destroyed by fire in one single catastrophic event. Several explanations have been put forward to explain the cause of this destruction layer, such as the deliberate demolition of old buildings during Roman redevelopment of the site after the revolt and also the possibility of an industrial process causing a large fire. Despite the existence of these quite credible possibilities, it is a very unlikely proposition that the Boudican rebels confined their activities to the north side of the river and chose not to cross the bridge, thus allowing the southern side of the settlement to remain unscathed. It would have made no sense at all to wreak such terrible and thorough devastation on one side of the river and then leave the other side, along with the vitally important bridge, intact. Unfortunately however, although there is no doubt that early Roman Southwark suffered some form of catastrophe and was burned to the ground, no evidence has yet come to light to support the suggestion that the bridge was also destroyed at the time of the revolt.

In the final analysis though, the evidence is compelling enough at least to strongly suggest that Boudica and her rebel army put the entire town to the torch, and may also have destroyed the bridge before advancing on Verulamium, thereby denying the Romans any opportunity to send rapid military assistance north of the Thames.

5

VERULAMIUM AND BEYOND

THE ORIGINS OF VERULAMIUM

The original settlement on which the modern town of St Albans is founded was first known by its native ancient British name of Verlamion, or to give it its approximate translation, 'the town above the marsh'. It was established in the first century BC during the reign of King Tasciovanus of the Catuvellauni tribe. Tasciovanus subsequently made the town his tribal capital, or *oppidum*, and it was his son Cunobelinus who, as has been discussed in an earlier chapter, was finally to succeed in taking permanent control of the old Trinovantean capital at Camulodunum, or Colchester as we are now more familiar with it today. The seizure and occupation of the site was an achievement which Tasciovanus himself had only ever managed on a temporary level some years before when he took brief control of it during his aggressive campaigns to increase the lands under the rule of his tribe. This was a policy which continued under the reign of the next great Catuvellaunian ruler, Cunobelinus, and one which saw the Catuvellauni rise to become the most powerful and politically influential of the British tribes prior to the Roman invasion of AD 43.

It is believed that the Catuvellauni people were formed from a loose confederation of small tribal groups who were originally drawn together with the express purpose of defending against the first Roman military incursions into Britain led by a conquest-hungry Julius Caesar. This indicates that, at the time of the later Claudian invasion, the Catuvellauni tribe was a relatively new power compared to some of the other British tribes. The tribal confederation that was mustered to resist both of Caesar's attempts at invasion was led into battle on each of those occasions by a British warrior chieftain known as Cassivellaunus. Whilst the part this future king played in leading the resistance against Caesar is documented well enough, his own background is altogether more shadowy. The only real clues that can be used in an attempt to piece together a picture of Cassivellaunus are contained within the structure of his name and the writings of his adversary, Julius Caesar. Those clues are not only very few and far between, they are also subject to being caught up in the spin that Caesar customarily injected into his memoirs in order to achieve maximum personal acclaim, even from his British incursions which achieved very little for Rome and should be regarded as spectacular failures overall. Caesar was, after all, not only a great general and politician, he was also an incredibly talented self-publicist with a gift for glossing over some of his less successful exploits.

Although the origins and composition of the name Cassivellaunus are not entirely certain, it is believed that the name first recorded by Caesar may be made up of his given name, Vellaunus, and the name of the tribe that he originally hailed from, the Cassi. If such is the case then the original meaning of the tribal name Catuvellauni could translate as 'the followers of Vellaunus'. It is interesting to note that, in Caesar's writings concerning the second invasion of Britain in the *Gallic Wars*, he mentions receiving a deputation of nobles from various British tribes who wished to enter into a peace agreement. It would seem that, faced with a difficult choice, these tribal ambassadors preferred to form an alliance with Caesar, which they probably hoped would secure his protection against the growing threat of the ambitious and power-hungry Cassivellaunus. One of the British tribes mentioned in the passage is in fact the Cassi, which would suggest that, if the theory is correct concerning the composition of the name Cassivellaunus, he had decided to forsake the bosom of his own people and had set out instead to make his own personal mark on the world. Given the high degrees of power and wealth that his new tribe would subsequently come to possess, this appears to have turned out to be quite an astute decision.

From the time of Cassivellaunus onwards the royal lineage becomes somewhat obscured and it is uncertain whether the next clear ruler that appears in the Catuvellaunian line of succession, Tasciovanus, was the son or the grandson of the tribal founder. Tasciovanus himself became leader of the tribe around 20 BC and soon began to implement aggressive policies that would expand the lands and influence of his tribe, most notably by breaching the treaty that Cassivellaunus had long ago agreed with Caesar which, amongst other things, protected the Trinovantes, thereby sparking off a fresh bout of hostilities against the tribe.

As mentioned above, it was eventually Cunobelinus who, once and for all, seized control of Colchester during the clashes with the Trinovantes that followed the reopening of hostilities between the two tribes. Once Cunobelinus had made the town his own, he wasted no time in transferring his power base from Verlamion to his new seat at Camulodunum, no doubt intending to take full advantage of cross-channel trading opportunities, much improved now because of the town's relatively close proximity to the short sea crossing between Britain and Gaul. This prime location would also allow him the opportunity to better promote his political involvements overseas. For a while, the power that Verlamion had once enjoyed began to dwindle next to the powerful influence of the new royal court at Camulodunum. Then, around AD 40, Caratacus and Togodumnus, having grown tired of years of having to stomach the pro-Roman views held by certain members of their family, including their father Cunobelinus, finally returned home to their ancestral seat. There, installed in the old tribal capital, they nurtured their hatred and mistrust of Rome and put the town to a new use. It became a base from which to direct their expansionist operations against their neighbours, such as Verica of the Atrebates who, as we now know, was eventually forced to take flight to Rome to ask for help.

By the time of the Claudian invasion the old Catuvellaunian capital had once more become a centre of considerable power. Verlamion had been the home of two of the most redoubtable British princes to resist Rome, and when their initial resistance was shattered and one prince lay dead, the other became an elusive guerrilla leader. No longer strong enough to openly stand against the might of the conquering Romans, Verlamion fell into new hands as the invaders from over the sea buried it under their new buildings and even corrupted its name with their own language.

However, despite the old tribal capital disappearing under the Roman sprawl of Verulamium, its symbolic meaning to the tribespeople who later became involved in the rebellion would still be a potent one indeed. Although the two princes were now gone, the legacy of their resistance to Rome remained within living memory, along with the desire to take control of the seat of their defiance, and the further desire to wield control once more over the power bases of the old confederation. It would no doubt be imperative therefore, that Boudica would have quickly needed to seize these towns in order to secure the support of the Trinovantean and Catuvellaunian nobles. As the revolt spread, the manpower that they would be able to bring to the coming fight was going to be vital if she was ever going to succeed in crushing Paulinus and his army. Retaking control of the old capital was not just an additional chance for plunder and revenge; one could actually say that it also represented a crucial component to the success of the rebellion.

THE FALL OF ST ALBANS

For those families and individuals who were most at risk from the approaching rebel host, either immigrant settlers or Romanised Britons living in Verulamium at the time of the Boudican revolt, it must have seemed as though life in the thriving new Roman town had turned into an almost instant and totally unexpected nightmare. For the immigrants, no doubt, the thought of embarking on a plan to travel over from a far-off homeland to seek their fortune would now seem a very bad decision to have made. The new lives they had made for themselves in this distant and still largely untamed land were now in danger of being torn away from them. However, worse still was the position of the native Britons who had chosen to embrace the new culture and lifestyle of the invading Romans. This act of apparent capitulation and the abandonment of their culture was going to guarantee a very special type of hatred and disgust from those natives who, as Tacitus alluded to in his account, were now openly demonstrating their hatred of the occupying forces of Rome. His mention of Paulinus travelling through 'disaffected territory' illustrates perfectly well that word of the revolt's progress was widespread throughout the old tribal lands, and that the native Britons were beginning to get the first heady whiffs of once more regaining their freedom from Rome. Then as now the people would have begun to feel braver, perhaps confident enough to demonstrate their feelings against those who had aided the Romans and abandoned their own.

In more recent history, the world witnessed the wrath of the people of France and the Low Countries when all of those citizens who had done their best to get on with life under an occupying power suddenly got a fresh taste of liberty. Towards the end of the Second World War, as the occupying German forces withdrew, many of those suspected of collaborating with the Nazis were hunted out and punished by ordinary people. The penalty of summary street justice varied from women who had entertained occupying troops being stripped and having their heads shaved to public lynchings for those who had spied on and betrayed their compatriots. The penalties suffered by the Roman lackeys, then living in a much more savage and violent world, would no doubt have been far more extreme as the native Britons were driven by their own hereditary tribal loyalty. Even today, the loyalty of the pack on a grand scale is not only a societal requirement but also forms part of our very nature as human beings.

Having heard the awful news about Camulodunum and living in fear for what was to become of them, those now identified as pariahs perhaps felt a brief glimmer of hope as they witnessed Paulinus ride south down Watling Street. They would no doubt have prayed hard that he and his small force would pull off the impossible and halt the advancing rebels, sparing them from the fate they feared most. But, days later, their hearts would have sank as they saw Paulinus once more, travelling back up the great road and leading his column of cavalry. His small force was now swelled by the London garrison and by a miserable trail of weary refugees from London, all now dispossessed and ever fearful that the mob responsible for destroying their thriving community would catch up with them and slaughter them. Anxious now to put distance between himself and the rebel force, Paulinus would not have lingered long at St Albans, save to advise the population that they should evacuate the town and flee the mob while they still could. Having done that he would have made haste to move north to join his main force and begin the preparations for a major engagement with the rebels on his chosen ground.

As the column left the town behind and moved off up Watling Street its numbers would now be swelled by those who were astute enough to realise what price they would pay if they remained behind. The writing would clearly have been on the wall as the sorry-looking column of people from London carried its own particular form of confirmation to the citizens of Verulamium. It proved that the threat was not only very real but also that it was not very far away either. The time for lengthy deliberation had now passed and hard choices had to be made. With heavy heart, many would have joined the column, hoping to follow it to safety, away from the danger that would soon reach the town. The future was uncertain, but for now at least they were going to be safe.

With no prospect of Roman military intervention and with the impending arrival of the force of rebel Britons, it is extremely doubtful if any semblance of order would have remained amongst the remaining populace of Verulamium. It is easy to envisage a situation where widespread panic and looting took a hold, along with random beatings and killings to settle old scores, even before the arrival of the rebel host. The situation that developed at Verulamium would have been very different to that of Londinium and Camulodunum and, combined with other local considerations, tells quite a different story to the fate of both of the aforementioned unfortunate towns.

Perhaps the most obvious physical difference between the three targets is that Verulamium was protected by extensive perimeter defence works, consisting of some of the surviving previous fortifications installed by the Catuvellauni which had been upgraded by the presence of newer, more effective Roman defences. Such an extensive system would have made the town quite a different proposition to the two previous defenceless towns that had been destroyed by Boudica's mob. The combined protection of the old and new structures was substantial enough to have allowed Verulamium to mount a credible attempt at defending itself against the impending rebel assault. However, the opportunity to mount such a defence was apparently never taken and the town was left vulnerable.

One can only assume that Paulinus again quickly considered his options and decided to sacrifice the town in order to rejoin his waiting battle group and maximise the time available to plan for a large-scale battle. The limited military resources available to him would probably have drawn him to conclude that mounting any sort of defence would only delay the inevitable, and that the town would eventually fall given the size of the force that would soon assail it. Furthermore, a defence of the town to delay the rebel army's advance would merely result in an unnecessary loss of valuable troops who could be used to better effect when he felt more inclined to deploy them.

Whereas Tacitus mentions, and names, all three of the attacked towns in the *Annals*, Cassius Dio mentions none of the towns by name in his *Roman Histories* and says only that two Roman towns suffered destruction at the hands of the rebels. Whilst it is at first almost automatic to think that the two towns he refers to are Camulodunum and Londinium, the historian is more likely to be referring to Camulodunum and Verulamium. The reason for this is that Londinium, although an important trading centre, was according to Tacitus not actually ranked as a town, whereas Camulodunum and Verulamium were both officially recognised Roman settlements. Camulodunum, as we have discussed, was established as a *colonia* to house army veterans after military usage ended. The town carried the added status of being the first Roman provincial capital of Britannia. At the time of the Boudican revolt Verulamium itself held the status of *municipium*, a title which it had been granted in AD 50 and which conferred the right of Roman citizenship on its inhabitants.

Whatever else the reasons were for the attacks on Camulodunum and Londinium, their destruction was, as has been mentioned previously, also vitally important tactically in order to hamper troop landings close to the main road system and thereby much reduce the chance of Paulinus receiving assistance from hurriedly shipped-in reinforcements. However, this kind of tactical importance cannot realistically be ascribed to Verulamium. The only military benefit to be derived from pressing an assault home would be to loot its food supply and deny its stores to any enemy force that might have been pursuing the rebels. Consequently, the only other possible reason for Boudica to take it would be to restore it to the Catuvellauni, thereby securing their support in return for liberating their old tribal capital.

Whilst the idea of a wider alliance may seem unlikely to some it is worth remembering that, throughout history, some very unlikely coalitions have been formed to achieve a mutually beneficial end result. If ever there was time to draw the British tribes together then the expulsion of Roman forces and government would be a prime motivator. As Tacitus implies in the *Annals*, the Britons had been plotting the uprising for some time before it actually occurred, and on an inter-tribal level.

This train of thought becomes more apparent when one examines another, perhaps more interesting difference between St Albans and Boudica's previous two main targets. Unlike Colchester and London, St Albans does not appear to have fallen victim to the previous total destruction that the other targets suffered. Archaeological evidence would seem to indicate that, rather than being totally razed to the ground, sizeable portions of the town did in fact survive the fire. Of course, this could well be attributable to the fact that, with the majority of Romanised inhabitants gone and the prospect of plunder and killing vastly reduced, the rebels would have lacked the murderous motivation needed to level the town. However, since evidence exists for the destruction of farmsteads and homes around the town it could be argued that more selective destruction was occurring and that certain local families were being spared the loss of their property in return for their support. Although probably no longer an open way of life in the Roman-occupied towns and territories, the traditional system of clientage to the Celtic nobility would still have an active influence over many Britons. Those higher-born families who still carried a degree of power and influence with their tribespeople would be capable of bolstering the rebels' numbers with their clients – something which the nobility would be more inclined to do if their properties and interests remained unmolested.

THE PUSH NORTH

After St Albans fell and the rebel army had carried out whatever looting and destruction it saw fit, the Boudican host would have moved on to its next objective and it is here that archaeology begins to struggle in providing us with answers as to exactly where the rebel army went. It has been suggested by some that Boudica and her army travelled no further north than just beyond Verulamium, choosing instead to stay in the southern half of the country. One of the reasons for this proposal is that, as yet, no firm evidence of the infamous Boudican destruction layer has been discovered beyond that point. This does not mean, however, that one should necessarily conclude that the rebels did not decide to advance any further north than the area of Verulamium.

By far the biggest single sources of hard evidence for the activities of the rebels are the archaeological clues left under the attacked sites, and the search for these is where any modern investigation is likely to become somewhat problematic. The difficulty is that at the time of the revolt, the larger Roman towns or settlements that later grew along Watling Street between St Albans and the Midlands had either not yet been established or were no more than very small civilian settlements. Many of the towns were established a decade or so after the revolt and could not therefore sit on that much sought-after characteristic destruction layer, a presence which has so far allowed us to pinpoint the exact locations and extent of the attacked sites and thereby conclusively track the movements of the rebel force. In addition, on top of the difficulty of locating evidence for one-off catastrophic events such as extensive fire damage on smaller sites, it would also be more troublesome to determine whether that damage is related to an act of war or civil strife or whether it was caused by accidental means.

The discovery of fire damage to structures from Roman Britain is relatively common. A large number of domestic and industrial activities utilised fire and heat, and those processes, combined with their close proximity to buildings that were largely constructed from an assortment of combustible materials, meant that destruction by fire was an ever-present hazard. It should therefore logically follow that the smaller the site, the scarcer the signs are likely to be when it comes to determining whether or not something more sinister than accidental damage occurred.

In all, five Roman towns and settlements now sit on Watling Street between Verulamium and Venonis at High Cross, a predominantly civilian Roman settlement sited on the junction with Watling Street and the Fosse Way on the border between Warwickshire and Leicestershire. These five towns and settlements are Durocobrivis (now Dunstable, Bedfordshire), Magiovinium (Dropshort, Buckinghamshire), Lactodurum (Towcester, Northamptonshire), Bannaventa (Whilton Lodge, Northamptonshire), and Tripontium (Cave's Inn, Warwickshire).

It seems folly to conclude that, just because there is no evidence for deliberate destruction at these sites which can safely be attributed to the period of the revolt, the rebel force could not have travelled that far north up the country. In the absence of evidence at these sites, it seems more sensible to consider why there is such a distinct lack of evidence for the movement of the Boudican force along the immediate line of Watling Street.

If it is correct that Boudica sat down with other tribal representatives prior to the revolt and laid detailed plans in relation to the objectives she wished to achieve, her actions prior to reaching St Albans are likely to have been more tactically driven than has been previously credited. It must also follow that, like any other good commander in the field, she would have been constantly revising her plans to suit the prevailing situation. Whilst it is fair to say that, as a leader of such an apparently disparate group, she had already achieved much by this point, it is likely that she could not have acted alone in attaining the level of success she had gained so far. Like any other successful commander she would have needed reliable advisors and lieutenants to form a command-and-control group capable of devising and implementing strategies that would require adjustments as the campaign progressed and conditions changed. In addition, these changes could only be decided upon through the use of good intelligence gathering, a prime example of which was the apparent usage of such intelligence to achieve the destruction of the IX Hispana battle group, a victory that would have been very hard to achieve in anything less than a carefully planned engagement.

As Boudica and her forces advanced, she would have been gathering a steady flow of supporters who would swell her ranks as they were swept along by the excitement of joining the seemingly unstoppable army of fellow Britons that was finally going to deliver them from Roman rule. Many would have been ordinary people, tradesmen, farmers, peasants, and the like – the sort of people who traditionally formed the bulk of a tribal army in time of war. In addition there would have been the warrior elite and the nobles, many of whom still trained and remained equipped to fight out of the way of prying Roman eyes. These ranged from the younger ones, who were trained warriors but had perhaps only gained limited experience of combat, to the veteran campaigners, some who may even have seen the Romans land and then stood against them in the great opening battles. Eventually, when the might of the legions became too much to face in head-on conflict, they had adapted their methods, following men like the wily Caratacus and spending years fighting a guerrilla-style campaign against the advancing Roman forces. Perhaps they returned home only when their legendary leader had been betrayed to the Romans, and waited for the arrival of another day when they would once more be able to rise and fight.

Such seasoned warriors and leaders would have possessed a wealth of experience in fighting the Romans and they would have been indispensable to the furtherance of Boudica's plans. They knew the local terrain, they would be able to enlist substantial local support, and crucially they knew what it was to wage war against the most modern and powerful army in the world. They would have been in

1 Thomas Thorneycroft's statue of Boudica, on the banks of the River Thames near the Houses of Parliament. Although historically inaccurate, for many people it is the ultimate embodiment of the spirit of Boudica.

2 The Imperial Forum and Senate house, Rome: the heart of the power wielded by Rome and a location that would have been very familiar to Paulinus.

3 The figures on the tombstone relief of the Roman cavalryman Longinus. The stone was recovered at Colchester and is widely believed to have been pulled down by the Boudican rebels as they attacked the town. The relief shows a naked tribesman being ridden down by Longinus, contrary to the view that the Celtic practice of fighting naked had died out by the time of the Boudican revolt. Whilst it cannot be assumed that it depicts the killing of a British adversary, it is certainly contemporary evidence that the practice was still followed by Rome's northern enemies around the period of the revolt. The tombstone is now on display in the Castle Museum, Colchester.

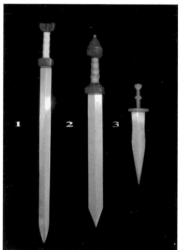

Above left: 4 Roman weapon types:
1. Standard-pattern *spatha* used by both auxiliary infantry and cavalry. The long slim blade is designed primarily for slashing and chopping.
2. Pompeii-pattern *gladius*. This broad, short blade with its strong, angular point is perfect for well-aimed thrusts at a variety of targets. Tests prove that the Pompeii style of blade is also capable of delivering devastating damage when used to chop or cleave.
3. *Pugio*. An iron-bladed dagger, in this case fitted with a heavy bronze handle. The broad, tapering blade and the weighty handle indicate that this weapon was primarily intended for stabbing rather than slashing.

Above right: 5 Native British tribes of the 1st century AD.

6 Castle Museum, Colchester. The imposing Norman keep was built directly over the remains of the great Roman temple dedicated to the Divine Claudius. Its foundations and vaults can still be viewed today in the castle undercrofts.

7 A slightly larger-than-life bronze head of the Emperor Claudius. It is widely accepted that the complete statue once stood in Camulodunum and was destroyed during the rebel attack on the town. The head was recovered in 1907 from the River Alde near Rendham in Suffolk, and was perhaps cast into the river as a votive offering. The original is now in the British Museum.

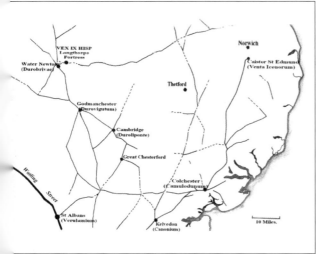

8 The main Roman roads in eastern Britain.

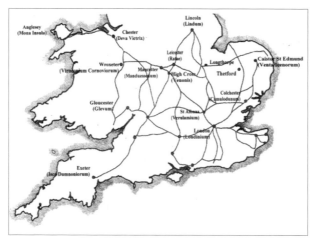

9 Southern Britain: main roads and key locations.

10 Located in the centre of modern Leicester, the Jewry Wall is all that remains of a late Roman bath house built to serve the tribal *civitas* of Ratae Coritanorum, administrative centre of the Coritani tribe.

11 Nestling in the heart of the Hampshire countryside, Butser Ancient Farm is an excellent example of the small farming communities typical of the lands of the Coritani tribe and Britain in general.

12 Quarry Lane, Mancetter. On the right is the Manor House, where work carried out to install a lamppost revealed evidence of the presence of the vexillation fortress.

13 The River Anker and surrounding area. The photograph was taken around 50 yards away from the supposed location of the eastern defences of Manduessedum fortress and looks roughly south-east towards the proposed Mancetter battle site. Note the pronounced rise in the land on the left. This is the direction towards which the Roman forces would have needed to make their advance.

14 The busy modern A5 (Watling Street) passing east through Smockington Hollow and up towards High Cross, which lies just beyond the horizon. This pronounced dip travels across much of the western edge of the High Cross plateau and is a credible candidate for the defile mentioned in the writings of Tacitus.

15 View approximately eastwards from the top of High Cross, towards the direction of the hypothetical rebel advance. This shot illustrates both the commanding view from the position and the ground sloping away towards the enemy.

Pilum Muralis.   Tribulus.

Section through ditch & rampart with Tribuli in place.

1 m

Left: 16 Roman ditch and rampart defence system.

Opposite above, left: 17 The proposed battlefield at High Cross, showing the theoretical distribution of Boudican and Roman forces and the location of possible flank defence works.

Opposite above, right: 18 Having advanced to within range of the Roman forward lines, the Britons sustain their first losses from a wave of *pila* thrown by the legionaries. Once the javelins have been thrown the forward lines of LEG XIIII then form wedges and burst into the charging Britons, splitting their forward ranks into smaller groups as they filter through the wedges. The auxiliary infantry move to attack the rebel flanks while the reserve legionary and cavalry formations move into position to prepare for the advance.

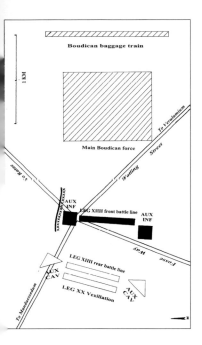

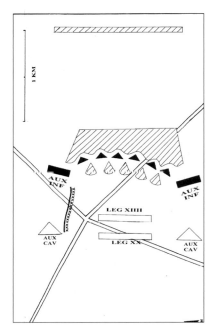

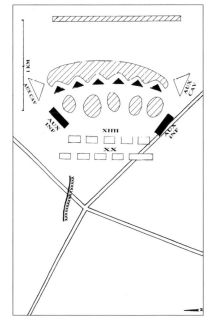

Right: 19 Whilst the legionary wedges push further into the main rebel force, the auxiliary infantry presses home attacks on both flanks, causing the Britons to fight on three sides. As the wedges cause the dense rebel formation to fragment, the rear formations from XIIII and XX Legions break into open-order cohort formations and charge down the hill into the smaller groups left by the advance of the wedges. The auxiliary cavalry then charges down either side of the battlefield and begins to attack the rear and flanks of the Boudican force.

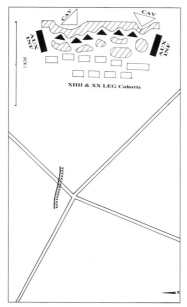

XIIII & XX LEG Cohorts

20 As the legionary wedges and auxiliary infantry continue to push into the main rebel formation, the rear legionary units charge down the slope engaging all of the smaller groups that have emerged from the other side of the forward assault. Not expecting the rapid and extremely violent Roman counter assault, many of the rebels begin to turn and run. Those who cannot escape are trapped by the line of the Boudican baggage train where, unable to flee, a massacre takes place as cavalry ranges up and down the line and the combined infantry group closes on the remaining rebels.

21 Boudica, the legend.

22 Figure A: Centurion.

23 Figure B: Legionary.

24 Figure C: Auxiliary infantryman.

25 Figure D: Auxiliary cavalryman.

26 Figure E: Icenian noble.

27 Figure F: British war chariot.

28 Figure G: Tribal Champion.

29 Figure H: The vexillation fortress at Mancetter.

a position to tell her how to inflict losses on the Roman army and survive to fight another day.

Now, in consultation with her new allies, she would need to decide on the correct course of action required to make progress beyond Verulamium. Boudica and her lieutenants would have known from their own experience that by travelling along the length of Watling Street they could be leaving their column open to the threat of ambush, just as they had lately surprised the IX Hispana. The rebels knew that somewhere ahead was Paulinus and, eventually, he was going to be in the company of the biggest force he could muster to counter her advance. Boudica's column would be slowly encroaching north in a disordered mass, nothing like the steady and ordered advance of a Roman marching column. If it followed Watling Street, it would be travelling on and either side of the road in a great vulnerable mass with its warriors mingled in here and there amongst the throng, in no particular order and penned in amongst a growing horde of followers.

The Britons had never practiced the ordered discipline so beloved of the Roman army. In addition, Britain had probably never seen a united tribal force of such size, so Boudica and her commanders would have realised that their lack of experience in leading such a large and diverse force would mean a likely inability to control its movements effectively. Therefore, exerting any sort of centralised order to create a more fluid advance would be pretty much impossible. It would also mean that, if Paulinus was able to launch an initial strike with a large fast-moving cavalry force, sent in first to inject panic and split up the mob, the resultant chaos could well spell disaster and the revolt would be finished. It is likely to have been the fear of this possibility that led Boudica and the other leaders to conclude that the safest method of travelling north would be to go across country, using local knowledge to move away from the road. This would allow her to range over a wide area, destroying isolated targets as she went. Civilian targets were all well and good for loot and plunder, but if isolated garrisons were cut off and destroyed during the advance she would achieve piecemeal destruction of the very forces that Paulinus might try to muster together to make a stand. Moreover, it would provide an opportunity to seize weapons, armour and food supplies that could be used both to strengthen the column and to deprive the enemy.

It is Cassius Dio this time who sheds some light on whether this was actually the option that Boudica chose to take. In one of the lengthy speeches he attributes to Boudica as she rouses her forces, he provides us with a reference to the Britons' ability to move across country and their familiarity with their surroundings:

> Our opponents, however, can neither pursue anybody, by reason of their heavy armour, nor yet flee; and if they ever do slip away from us, they take refuge in certain appointed spots, where they shut themselves up as in a trap. But these are not the only respects in which they are vastly inferior to us: there is also the fact that they cannot bear up under hunger, thirst, cold, or heat, as we can. They require shade and covering, they require kneaded bread and wine and oil, and if any of these things fails them, they perish; for us, on the other hand, any grass or root serves as bread, the juice of any plant as oil, any water as wine, any tree as a house. Furthermore, this region is familiar to us and is our ally, but to them it is unknown and hostile. As for the rivers, we swim them naked, whereas they do not across them easily even with boats. Let us, therefore, go against them trusting boldly to good fortune. Let us show them that they are hares and foxes trying to rule over dogs and wolves.
>
> (Cassius Dio, *Roman Histories* LXII.5)

Of course, Dio is nothing if not sensationalist in his style, and this may well be just another method he has employed to convey the barbarity of the Britons to his readers. By seemingly ignoring the well-documented resilience and toughness of the Roman fighting machine and deliberately playing up the more civilised aspects and cosseted lifestyles of Roman society, he presents a stark contrast to the image he desires to create of semi-wild barbarian Britons, savage people who are able to exist as one with their surroundings, seemingly without need of any of the comforts of more civilised people such as his well-bred Roman readership sitting in the comfort of their homes, villas and palaces.

In addition, there is a very brief mention in the earliest accounts given by Tacitus:

> The natives enjoyed plundering and thought of nothing else. Bypassing forts and garrisons, they made for where loot was richest and protection weakest.
>
> (Tacitus, *Annals* XIV.33)

Although these references are by no means conclusive in supporting the suggestion that the rebel force took a cross-country route, they serve in some small way to reinforce the notion that this option was at least feasible, more so when combined with the tactical considerations that have been mentioned earlier. Although Tacitus suggests that the Britons avoided forts and garrisons, were the Britons to have come across small garrisons whilst in sufficient strength to take them on it is unlikely that the Roman troops would have been spared their attentions. At any rate, the suggestion seems to be that the Britons were ranging over a wide area in search of targets, perhaps not confining themselves to the course of a road particularly.

If one accepts, either as a matter of course or on the basis of the above discussion, that the Boudican force could well have decided to travel north then the next question that begs an answer would be: why would Boudica want to bring her force any further north?

6

THE FOX AND THE EAGLE

COST VS REWARD

In making the decision to push north, Boudica would have been fully aware that she would be taking herself and her army ever closer to much larger concentrations of Roman troops than she had so far had to do battle with. On reaching Verulamium she had achieved the destruction of two large Roman population centres and vanquished a force representing over half the strength of a full legion. She and her rebels had no doubt also torn apart any small isolated garrisons and settlements that they had located along the route. But the military strength that she would soon be likely to encounter was going to be much stronger than of these.

Directly to the north of her, Petilius Cerialis would be licking his wounds with the remainder of the IX Hispana Legion, no doubt under orders from Paulinus and bolstered with strategically placed garrisons of auxiliary troops. Cerialis and his soldiers would now be securing the territory that marked the eastern half of the northern buffer zone between the Roman-occupied territories and the northern tribes such as the Brigantean confederation and the Parisi. The extent of that half of the zone covered much of what is now Leicestershire, Nottinghamshire and Lincolnshire.

To the north-west of the Boudican army lay a greater threat still, in the form of the extensively garrisoned region of the central and northern Midlands which also took in the lands stretching over towards the borders of Wales, beyond which lay the wild Welsh tribes such as the Demetae, the Ordovices and the Deceangli who occupied the areas of central and northern Wales. In this central area lay the Roman military bases most likely to act as staging points for Paulinus to group his forces and prepare his strategy for engaging the rebel army in battle.

During the early years of the Roman occupation, the central and western Midlands saw a great deal of fighting as the Romans pushed westwards from their first great frontier line, a boundary which had been marked by the line of the Fosse Way as it made its way up from the West Country towards Lincolnshire. It is very likely that, while the XX Legion cut a swathe directly across the centre of the country to take control of the territory around Gloucestershire and Hereford, the XIIII Gemina Legion fought its way across the top of the region, cutting a path through the lands of the Coritani, pushing into the home territories of the Cornovii, and then thrusting on further still to the areas west of Shropshire and Worcestershire, before eventually arriving in Cheshire. The eventual aim of the thrust west would be to amass a much larger force of legionaries and auxiliary units on the tribal border lands for the push into the lands of the Welsh tribes. As the legions completed each stage of their advance they built roads, large fortresses, smaller forts and supply depots all over the areas that they had subjugated, which eventually formed a network of bases that allowed them to exercise tight military control of the newly acquired territories. It was a little like establishing a large central police station and then building local sub-stations to maintain control of specific areas while the main station assumed responsibility for overall administration of the region. This network of roads and bases, which included the westward extension of Watling Street from its junction with the Fosse Way, was now facilitating the progress of the XIIII Gemina Legion as they marched back from Anglesey to join their commander, Paulinus as he made ready for battle.

For Boudica and her rebel leaders, now would be a time to make choices, and quickly. Boudica would urgently need to give the rebel army a new objective in order to maintain cohesion and momentum, but she would also need to make sure that her decision was not going to be beyond the capabilities of her army. She could not realistically stay where she was and try to coax Paulinus back down Watling Street as a delay might mean facing an attack on two fronts. As we have already seen in one of the extracts from the accounts of Tacitus, reinforcements were subsequently sent over from bases in Germany in sufficient strength to have posed a real problem if they had arrived in time to catch up with and engage the rebel army. North or north-west was the only option left open if Boudica and her rebels were to avoid these forces, but they would then be faced with the prospect of coming across and engaging a far larger force of battle-hardened Roman troops, who would be much more prepared for her than previously when she took on the unwitting Cerialis and the now devastated battle group of the IX Hispana Legion.

Traditionally, when the story of Boudica is recounted, it is delivered as a tale of bloody revenge for the wrongs heaped upon her by the occupying Romans. The popular explanation for the revolt is that it was motivated only by righteous indignation and a burning desire for retribution. The ready assertion always seems to be that, having embarked on a frenzied orgy of murder, pillage and destruction, Boudica and her followers made straight for the Roman forces for one last big showdown to settle the matter once and for all. The simplest supporting argument for this version of events is going to be that the rebellious Britons were extremely buoyed up by their earlier successes. Knowing that they were immensely numerically superior to the force under Paulinus's command, Boudica and the rebel mob would have no doubt made the decision that they could confidently launch an attack that would squash the last of the life out of their Roman tormentors, and that once victory was theirs they would be free once more. History tells us that Boudica grossly underestimated the superior fighting ability of the opposing Roman force and this in turn led to their last great push for freedom being doomed to failure.

If one instead accepts that the outrages of Decianus were actually a catalyst for the formulation of a more considered and deliberate strategy, and that the victories subsequently won by the rebels were not just the lucky results of a disorganised rampage through the countryside but are evidence of the effectiveness of a large British tribal coalition, the more popular version of events has to be called into question. In addition, this more popular version is definitely at variance with the next assertion to be made, that there was a much more reasoned motivation to take the route north than simply that the rebel army was spoiling for a fight.

As we have discussed in a previous chapter, far from angling for an early engagement with Paulinus and throwing her rebel force into a major battle, Boudica first wished to make certain that she had all the available support she could muster in order to obliterate the Roman army which would eventually be ranged against her. By travelling from St Albans in a straight north-westerly course across the land rather than the road, Boudica could, by spreading her forces out, both reduce the chance of engaging in any major entanglements with the enemy before she was ready and shorten the distance to her next big objective. If she achieved this objective, she could potentially cement another crucial tribal alliance and ultimately finish up in control of by far the greatest combined tribal force that ancient Britain had ever seen. As if that was not impressive enough, the alliances she had forged would ensure that, if this final step was successful, the entire eastern half of Roman-occupied territory north of the Thames would be totally under her control. But, in order to achieve this, she would first have to take the *civitas* of Ratae Coritanorum.

THE SIGNIFICANCE OF RATAE

Today it exists as the city of Leicester, but in the first century AD Ratae Coritanorum was the administrative capital of the Coritani people, and just like the other tribal centres of the southern half of Roman Britain it was securely under Roman control. However, unlike the previous tribal centres of power that fell under the advance of the Boudican force, Ratae was not regarded as the true capital, or *oppidum*, of the tribe. The tribal lands of the Coritani were extensive, taking in the modern counties of Lincolnshire, Nottinghamshire and Leicestershire, as well as some parts of Derbyshire and South Yorkshire to the north and a small portion of Northamptonshire to the south. It is possibly due to this extensive geographical spread that the tribe was apparently divided up into a maximum of three regional governments. Each sub-region had its own ruler who would be responsible for local administration, but all of the sub-groups would be presided over by a supreme overlord.

Although existing as one large tribe, the Coritani were most probably made up of a conglomerate of smaller tribal units who eventually elected to band themselves together under a common name and rulership, possibly in response to the ever-present threat of aggression from the larger, more powerful neighbouring tribes. The Coritanian people were essentially made up of scattered agricultural communities of largely peaceable folk who, unlike their neighbours, shunned the use of the more traditional established tribal communities such as hill forts and larger settlements with big populations. In addition, as we have discussed, the Coritani made no real attempts to resist the occupation of their lands by the Romans, perhaps choosing instead to capitalise on the deterrent effect that the Roman military presence would have in preventing any future incursions by their neighbours.

In AD 44 the Coritanian settlement that stood on the site at Ratae was captured by the rapidly advancing Roman forces and by

AD 50 the settlement had been buried under a legionary vexillation fortress, blotted out in effect in the same manner as Camulodunum and Verulamium. The site of the former tribal settlement would eventually develop into a major Roman city which, at its greatest, sprawled across nearly 100 acres of land. By the time of the Boudican revolt the site had already become the new tribal centre, or *civitas*, which served as the base for the Roman regional administration of the Coritani tribe. As such it would have represented no less an attractive target to the rebels than those they had previously attacked. The nearest major Roman base to Ratae was located a good day's march away at Manduessedum, which is now the site of Mancetter in north Warwickshire, and Ratae was also conveniently distant from the military bases under the control of the Roman troops serving under Cerialis's command. Additionally, Ratae no longer accommodated such a large legionary garrison as the one previously stationed in the old Claudian vexillation fortress. The legionaries and their bases had been moved further north to maintain a grip on those territorial gains closest to the northern limits of Roman occupation, and the town was probably now garrisoned by just a small force of auxiliary troops.

If, as has been discussed earlier in this work, Boudica had met to conspire with leaders from the major tribes that neighboured her own lands prior to the revolt, then it is feasible to suggest that the price stipulated for enlisting the support of the Coritani was the requirement of the rebel force to advance on the town and wipe out the Roman administration in the area. This would then destabilise the Roman grip on the tribe. If this could be achieved then perhaps even the supreme ruler of the Coritani at the time would return to his homelands and subsequently lend his support on the ground to strengthen the rebel alliance.

A ruler known as Volisios is the man most likely to have been the last of the overlords of the Coritani who had left, along with his three sub-rulers, as the Romans arrived in his lands. We know of him and the names of his sub-rulers, Dumnovellaunus, Dumnocoveros and Cartivelios, through coin finds which have turned up not only in their own tribal lands but also in the territory of the neighbouring Parisi tribe.

If the rebels had achieved all their objectives, thereby persuading the Coritani to join their ranks, Boudica would then have successfully secured the support of all of the tribes of much of the eastern quarter of southern and central Britain. This would particularly be the case if the self-exiled Coritanian nobles were able in turn to enlist the support of the Parisi.

Occupying what is now the East Riding of Yorkshire, the Parisi were one of the smaller British tribes. They were, at the time of the revolt, living in lands just beyond the limits of the Roman occupation zone, and in whose lands the higher members of the Coritanian nobility had sought refuge once they had fled their homelands. It seems reasonable to suggest that the Parisi would have taken very little persuading to join the revolt, in the eventuality that Ratae fell into the hands of the rebels. It must not have taken a great deal of foresight for the Parisi to realise that the Roman forces were just a small push away from entering their lands, and that only by joining the rebellion could an incursion realistically be prevented from happening once the Romans had found a suitable excuse to mount an attack upon them.

THE DRUIDIC QUESTION

So far in this work the subject of the Druids has remained largely unexamined, and it is not really the aim of this book to offer any in-depth discussion into what is a complex and at times obscure subject matter. Any examination of the mechanics of the Boudican revolt, however, would seem incomplete without a brief visit into the world of the Druid priesthood and at least attempting to form some sort of picture of their possible contribution to the rebellion.

In classical texts, many accounts exist of Druid priests and their practices and beliefs, but it is perhaps Julius Caesar's clear descriptions of the Druids of Britain and Gaul that best illustrate their status and purpose:

> Everywhere in Gaul there are only two classes of men who are of any account or consideration. The common people are treated almost as slaves and never venture to act on their own initiative, and are not consulted on any subject. Most of them, crushed by debt or heavy taxation, or the oppression of more powerful persons, bind themselves to serve men of rank, who exercise over them all the rights that masters have over slaves. The two privileged classes are the Druids and the knights. The Druids officiate at the worship of the gods, regulate public and private sacrifices and give rulings on all religious questions. Large numbers of young men flock to them for instruction, and they are held in great honour by the people. They act as judges in practically all disputes, whether between tribes or individuals; when any crime is committed, or a murder takes place, or a dispute arises about an inheritance or boundary, it is they who adjudicate the matter and appoint the compensation to be paid and received by the parties concerned. Any individual or tribe failing to accept their award is banned from taking part in sacrifice – the heaviest punishment that can be inflicted upon a Gaul. Those who are under such a ban are regarded as impious criminals. Everyone shuns them and avoids going near or speaking to them, for fear of taking some harm by going near what is unclean. If they appear as plaintiffs, justice is denied them, and they are excluded from taking a share in any honour. All of the Druids are under one head, whom they hold in the highest respect. On his death, if any one of the rest is of outstanding merit then he succeeds to the vacant place. If several have equal claims, the Druids usually decide the election by voting, though sometimes they actually fight it out. On a fixed date in each year they hold a session in a consecrated spot in the lands of the Carnutes, which is supposed to be the centre of Gaul. Those who are involved in disputes assemble

here from all parts and accept the Druids' judgement and awards. The Druidic doctrine is believed to have been found existing in Britain and then imported to Gaul; even today those who want to make a profound study of it generally go to Britain for the purpose.

(Julius Caesar, *Gallic Wars* VI. 13)

Caesar's description sets out for us not only some of the main roles and extent of the power enjoyed by the Druids, but also the different levels of society under which both the Gauls and their British cousins across the channel lived. Many of the more southerly tribes of Britain were in fact directly descended from Gaulish tribes of the same name, for example the various tribal groups of the Belgae. They too lived in a strong societal order which was dominated both morally and spiritually by the Druids, a priesthood which was clearly very powerful and also influential enough to overturn even royal decrees if they saw fit. It is clear from this account that the Druidic heritage of Britain was very important to the history and tradition of the wider European Celtic community, and seems to have been regarded as the spiritual home of the priesthood by the continental tribes.

There are those today who take the view that Caesar's descriptions of the Druids and their practices are inaccurate and at times fanciful. Perhaps it could be argued that certain elements do not tally with what is now known of the Druids, but on the whole it is unwise to treat his accounts of the priesthood with too much suspicion. Whilst Caesar was a first-class self-publicist and spin doctor, it cannot be denied that he was a learned man who made the effort to accurately describe the world around him as he experienced it. Since he also held high religious offices, we can perhaps also attribute to him a desire to understand what made the faith of others so different to his own. And of course there was his friendship with the Aeduan leader Diviciacus, a man whom he clearly held among the highest levels of esteem and trust. From Diviciacus Caesar would have learned much about the ways of the people who were then steadily falling under his control. It is thus perhaps Caesar's contemporary accounts of the priesthood which best assist us in understanding why the Romans came to regard the Druids as a serious threat to their administration, and why, having first imposed proscription over membership of the priesthood in Gaul, they carried the idea further in Britain and systematically began to wipe the order out.

In general, the Romans were tolerant of any native religions which did not pose any apparent threat to the Roman state. As the extent of their control spread over the length and breadth of the ancient world, they assimilated many local religions into their own practices and beliefs. However, what the Romans would not tolerate was the continuing influence of a revered body of priests whom they perceived as holding a greater power over their native subjects than the new, ordered and civilised Roman administration. So, rather than outlaw the religion of the Druids, they first outlawed membership of the Druidic order itself. When that failed, they hunted them down and slaughtered them. As Britain was clearly a seat of great Druidic power and tradition, it would be there that the Romans directed their efforts at eradication of the priesthood most fiercely. Their campaign would eventually lead them to the western extremities of the once mysterious land, where they would storm and destroy the sanctuaries and sacred groves of Mona.

Of the many distasteful practices that the Romans hated about Druidism, possibly the worst was ritualistic human sacrifice. Such rituals had no place in traditional Roman beliefs and the idea was generally abhorrent to the Romans, who determined to stamp out such a vile and uncivilised practice. Whilst the significance of headhunting within Celtic society has already been touched on, human sacrifice carried a far greater religious importance. As both Tacitus and Cassius Dio claim, this practice was responsible for many deaths after the fall of the towns that were destroyed during the revolt. Both historians, particularly Cassius Dio, make mention of this practice to illustrate the wild and barbarous nature of the rebel Britons; however, the slaughter of prisoners after a battle would have been a vitally important religious custom to the Britons, and not necessarily, as the Roman historians would have us believe, purely an act of cruel revenge.

As seen earlier, Tacitus mentions in the *Annals* that the Britons did not take prisoners or exchange them, choosing instead to kill them. Cassius Dio adds to this by describing, in graphic detail, the butchery that the Britons are alleged to have performed. Interestingly, however, he also mentions that much of this killing was carried out in the sacred groves of the Britons, and particularly in the groves of Andate, goddess of victory. Whilst today we find such practices uncivilised and abhorrent, as no doubt would the original Roman readers of the work, to the Britons it was a fulfilment of a promise. Before they launched their attacks they would have prayed to the gods from whom they sought favour and dedicated a solemn vow that, if the gods granted that they were victorious in battle, those of the enemy still left alive would be sacrificed by way of thanks for bestowing victory on their endeavours. What Tacitus or Dio fail to mention is that the Britons would have also have sacrificed captured horses and livestock as part of that same ritual.

This ritual behaviour would have been carried out by the victorious Britons as a matter of course in order to continue to receive the support of their gods. It was a ritual of blood that would have taken place, in one form or another, at every site where Boudica and the rebels had prevailed. To them this was merely the most appropriate and reverent thing to do when thanking the gods for their support, and it would have been the Druids who taught these rites to their people through generation after generation. However much we, with our modern sensibilities, may now deplore their seemingly brutal actions, we must at least try to understand that their chief motivation was faith and not bloodthirsty vengeance.

As well as the observation, control and implementation of religious ritual, Caesar also tells us that the Druids frequently mediated amongst individuals and tribes and passed judgements which could overrule even the word of the nobility. Such powerful people would have been indispensable at any gathering to discuss how best to rise up against the Romans. Their universally revered status would have been crucial if those clandestine meetings had contained parties or individuals who would otherwise not normally stand any chance of reaching an accord. The power of the Druidic order was hugely influential and could reach beyond the restrictions of personal and tribal enmity, thereby helping to facilitate agreements which may never otherwise have came about. Once the details had been agreed upon it would again be the Druids who could act as neutral messengers to enlist further support for what was about to happen. They would know which tribes would be most prepared to get involved, and it would have been in their own best interests to make the mission succeed, before the Romans finally hunted them down and exterminated them completely.

Could it be, therefore, that having scattered the seeds of the revolt and promoted the idea of tribal unity to achieve the ultimate goal, the Druids sheltering on Mona simply ran out of time and luck, and the distraction of the revolt itself came just too late to save them? Could it also be that their power was ultimately able to bring about a situation in the south-west of the province that would serve to deny Paulinus the chance of receiving reinforcements, and lead to the camp prefect of an illustrious legion taking his own life?

POENIUS POSTUMUS & II AUGUSTA – SHAMING THE EAGLE?

Poenius Postumus was in command of the II Augusta Legion at the time of the Boudican revolt. The legion was then stationed in the fortress at Isca Dumnoniorum, now Exeter in Devon. Postumus was the *praefectus castrorum* or camp prefect of the legion, and the part he was to play in the story of the revolt would eventually lead him to a personal catastrophe which would not only cost him his life but would also result in a stain on his personal and professional reputation which still endures after nearly two millennia. The reason for Postumus's downfall was that he failed to act on a critical order sent by Paulinus. The despatch required him, presumably in the absence of the Legate, to send troops north urgently. These badly needed reinforcements, had Postumus decided to obey the order and send them, would then have been used to bolster the force that the Governor Paulinus was assembling to confront Boudica and her rebel army.

There exists only one classical account of the affair, in the *Annals* of Tacitus. In a terse, almost contemptuous passage towards the end of his description of the revolt, Tacitus mentions what he perceives as the disgraceful failure of Postumus:

> Poenius Postumus, camp prefect of the Second Legion which had not joined Paulinus, learning of the success of the other two formations, stabbed himself to death because he had cheated his legion of its share in the victory and broken regulations by disobeying his commander's orders.
>
> (Tacitus, *Annals* XIV.37)

It seems from this short and very accusatory passage that Postumus was considered damned in the memory of Rome. He would have to take his place in history as a coward, who, having received word of the success of the rebel forces, apparently decided that it would be safer to ignore the order of his commander and remain within the safety of his fortress.

Other than his name, and the position he held at the time of the revolt, nothing is known of the life of Postumus. However, it seems very difficult to believe that a man in his position, who had attained the rank he had within his legion, would be in any way inclined to fail his governor at the crucial moment and instead elect to commit a gross act of cowardice at the prospect of facing the enemy. Unlike the young tribunes who were drawn from the privileged classes of the Roman nobility, doing their bit in the army before ascending the *cursus honorum*, Postumus achieved his hard-won rank by fighting his way up the ladder from the very bottom rung. Finally he had achieved the pinnacle of his career, no doubt in middle age or later, after many hard years of proving himself worthy through successive promotions. He would certainly have served at every level between legionary and his current position; this would have included the ranks of the centurionate, an officer corps which, by the very nature of their battlefield duties, suffered quite a high mortality rate. There are many today who attempt to place a modern equivalent alongside the rank of centurion, but there is no real equivalent if it is looked at merely as a general title. The centurionate was made up of many levels of seniority, and those men who were good enough to attain the rank held a great number of roles not only within the organisation of the legions but also in auxiliary formations.

Postumus's career would have seen him achieve total competence in all of these various roles and levels of authority. The wealth of experience that he thus developed would culminate in his proving himself to be the absolute best amongst an elite group of very tough and experienced leaders. His hard-won extensive knowledge and skill would have been so respected that, upon attaining the rank of *praefectus castrorum*, he would even have been in a position to offer advice and guidance to his superiors. His counsel would be invaluable and respected given that it had been drawn from practical, sometimes bitter, experience and was therefore something that would not be taken lightly.

In order to form a clearer picture of Postumus, it will be easier to assume that he served throughout his career within the various centuries and cohorts of the II Augusta. Whilst it is known that many centurions' careers included service in a number of different legions, there were also those who spent their entire length of service in one unit. Perhaps it would not be too far from the truth to say that the revered position of *praefectus castrorum* was an appointment that would have been more fitting for someone who had spent his entire time with the legion, and thus knew its makeup inside out.

If Postumus had indeed always served with the II Augusta then his service history would have been quite remarkable. By virtue of the likely time taken to achieve his rank, he would actually have sailed over in the Claudian invasion fleet. Perhaps at that time he was serving as an *optio* or junior centurion, and after the initial landings he continued to serve his legion, spending many years fighting in some of the most ferocious battles and campaigns that the Roman army waged for control of the south and south-west of Britain.

The II Augusta Legion was probably established in late Republican times. It was later reconstituted during Augustus's reforms of the army, hence its name and its subsequent adoption of the Capricorn emblem, a symbol to which Augustus attributed great luck and which is synonymous with the legions that were established during his reforms. At the time of the invasion of Britain it was selected, along with other legions and a large force of auxiliary cavalry and infantry, to join the invasion force that was massing on the coast of Gaul at the town of Portus Itius, now the French seaport of Boulogne. The II Augusta was mobilised from its base at Argentoratum, now Strasbourg in the Alsace region of France. It then became one of four legions which took part in the invasion of AD 43.

The legion subsequently spent the early years of the occupation fighting its way across the south of the country, initially under the command of the future Emperor Vespasian, a man regarded as a brilliant campaigner and renowned for his expertise in the use of artillery. The mastery of the use of these deadly machines was a talent which proved useful time and again as the legion engaged in often extremely difficult and vicious fighting for control of a string of defended settlements and hill forts, including the sprawling and seemingly impregnable Maiden Castle in Dorset. The legion fought in over thirty battles, operating for years in separate detachments garrisoned in a network of forts scattered across the southern counties and the West Country. The II Augusta finally regrouped into one large force and established its first permanent base in Britain at Exeter in AD 48, where it remained until it was transferred to Gloucester in AD 67.

It was at the great fortress at Isca Dumnoniorum that Postumus most probably received those fateful orders from Paulinus, directing him to send troops to his aid. If we are to assert that Postumus did not deliberately fail his governor then we must provide more evidence than the probable high quality of his character, his personal integrity and his excellent service record in an attempt to vindicate him.

By the time of the revolt, Isca had access to the extensive Roman road system, and any force that Postumus could have despatched would have joined the road leading to the Fosse Way for the march north. Due to the grave situation faced by Paulinus, the prefect would have probably received orders to send at least 2,000 troops if their support was going to be anywhere near adequate, and the soldiers would have been forcing the pace to reach their rendezvous point with the main body of Paulinus's force. If the vexillation from II Augusta remained on the line of the Fosse Way they would have eventually reached its junction with Watling Street at High Cross which, as previously mentioned, is around a day's march from Ratae Coritanorum. The total distances and times for the journey are as follows:

Isca Dumnoniorum to Venonis = 205 Roman miles.
Marching time at forced pace of 25 Roman miles per day = 8.2 days' march.

(Distances are again based on the use of modern routes.)

Paulinus would have been aware of how much time it would have taken for the reinforcements to have covered the distance between their base and the junction at High Cross, the relevance of which we will explore in greater detail in a later chapter. The likelihood is that he therefore sent for them either at the time of making his appraisal of the situation at Londinium or very soon after, in order to give the requested troops sufficient time to march up from the West Country. As well as ordering the II Augusta to move, Paulinus would also have ordered the XX Legion to send a vexillation. He would then have sent word to his main force, comprising the XIIII Gemina and associated auxiliary units, to move to a holding position, which he would probably have reconnoitred and chosen whilst travelling south along Watling Street to Londinium.

Paulinus's orders for extra manpower would have needed to be based on his personal understanding of the current situation in the province as a whole, and he would therefore have had to calculate carefully how many troops he could safely take from other legion garrisons. Given the apparent volatility of the tribes not yet involved in the revolt, he would have had to take great care to ensure that the abstraction of the reinforcements he required would not only be sufficient to support the troops going into battle against the rebels, but would also not result in destabilising the areas from which he was drawing them. If he took too many troops he risked seeing the partial or even total collapse of Roman control over potentially hostile territory. The lands currently under the control of the Roman military were home to tribes which may well have felt inclined to seize the opportunity that now presented itself. After all, the occupied tribes would have drawn the obvious conclusion that the Romans would never again be as weak as they were now, and that consequently the time was right to rise up in rebellion. If all of this was to be avoided then it was paramount that a visible deterrent be maintained during the emergency. Conversely, if Paulinus asked for too few then he might well lose the coming fight, and if any of the Roman units managed to survive the battle they would certainly not last much longer after the main fight was over.

Only the shrewdest of tacticians was going to be capable of pulling the situation back from the brink now, and Paulinus would have been acutely aware that every decision he made would have to be the right one. With that in mind, it is perhaps at this juncture that he apparently misread the situation in the tribal regions policed from

Isca Dumnoniorum, and subsequently made the mistake of asking for more assistance than one of his commanders could give.

It has recently come to light that, far from being in a position where he could afford to release a contingent of his troops to support Paulinus, Poenius Postumus may well have been facing an emergency in his own jurisdiction which would have made it impossible for him to release any of his men as reinforcements. Archaeologists are beginning to uncover evidence which may suggest that some form of tribal unrest was going on in the area of Somerset, then a newly occupied zone controlled by the II Augusta, around the same time that Boudica and her followers had risen up in rebellion. If such was the case then Postumus would have needed all of his men to contain the situation, and this would obviously mean that sending much-needed troops north would leave him dangerously overstretched.

An example of the type of unrest that Postumus may have faced in his jurisdiction has been unearthed at Cadbury Castle, a large, imposing hill fort which rises to 500 feet above sea level and dominates the area of the Somerset levels close to the village of South Cadbury. Dramatic evidence uncovered by archaeologists now illustrates a particularly bloody episode in the history of this ancient site which provides stark proof of a devastating attack and subsequent slaughter of its occupants by besieging Roman forces.

At first it was believed that the now infamous massacre layer was linked to the post-invasion campaigns of Vespasian as he pushed across the southern end of Britain. However, it now appears that the earlier interpretation of dating evidence was in fact incorrect and that the actual date of the massacre at South Cadbury could be attributable to the time of the Boudican revolt. Excavation work carried out on the south-west gateway of Cadbury Castle paints an incredible picture of a brutally effective attack carried out by Roman forces on the great hill fort. It appears that the native defenders failed to repel the Roman assault and instead succumbed to fire and sword. Evidence has been uncovered of an intense blaze and the remains of men, women and children left scattered around unburied, to be preyed upon by wild animals. Amongst the bodies lie the weapons and armour fragments of both the native British defenders and the Roman assault force, including ominous evidence of the use of deadly Roman siege artillery in the form of iron bolt tips.

It may be that, in the overall scheme of things, whatever unrest was taking place in Somerset did not pose too much of a problem to the troops based in the area. While still at full strength they could deal with the problem effectively and prevent things from spreading. The main problems would come if they were subsequently reduced in strength and were not then able to keep such a tight lid on the situation. If the Roman grip was then loosened and the unrest took a greater hold then it would have the potential to escalate further as Britons in the surrounding areas took heart from the Roman's apparent inability to suppress things effectively and took up arms against them. Such a projection could well have been made by Postumus, providing him with sufficient reason to make the fateful decision to deny Paulinus his much-needed men, extremely reluctantly one would imagine.

The area administered from Isca Dumnoniorum was extensive, and the fortress formed the hub for a number of smaller forts which extended their control across the neck of the South-West peninsula, stretching over from the coast of western Dorset towards Bridgewater Bay and the mouth of the Severn. With the legion fortress acting as a central depot and command post, the smaller forts would have had responsibility for patrolling their own areas and maintaining control over the local tribespeople. The tribe which occupied these lands was the Dumnonii, who covered the entire peninsula from Land's End up to the further reaches of Somerset; here they were bordered by the Durotriges, a people occupying an area roughly represented by the modern county of Dorset.

The Dumnonii had traded with Rome for years before the occupation and the tin they mined was a commodity in great demand by the Romans, who used it chiefly to make bronze. Whilst the Dumnonii were happy enough to engage in a long-standing trade agreement with Rome, it seems that playing host to the Romans as an occupying force was not something the tribe ever embraced with any great enthusiasm. Even after the Romans had gained a foothold in their territories and had firmly established themselves in other parts of Britain, the Dumnonii apparently had little time for the ways of their occupiers. They steadfastly refused to be Romanised and doggedly maintained their traditional way of life by shunning the newly imported version of civilisation that the Romans established, continuing instead to live in traditionally built settlements, carrying on with their own customs and practices and distancing themselves from the new Britain that grew beyond their lands.

It is striking to note that the lands of the Dumnonii exhibit a complete absence of the urbanisation that became a characteristic of Roman occupation in other parts of the province. Apart from a handful of remote outposts, the marked lack of Roman sites such as the forts, towns and settlements that were elsewhere dotted around most of the province makes the Dumnonian lands look more like the unconquered regions of the Highlands of Scotland. The lands of the Dumnonii were wild and remote. Even today much of it remains largely untouched, including such areas of unspoilt natural beauty as Dartmoor, Exmoor and Bodmin Moor. Wonderfully spiritual lands which are still as wild as the people who once roamed them, they lie under damp mists and low rolling clouds, largely unspoilt by modern intrusion – beautiful on the one hand, but even today incredibly dangerous to the unwary visitor. The ancient legacy of the Dumnonii still echoes in the more secluded, rural parts of Devon and Cornwall in the form of enduring ancient customs and practices which are a direct link to the Celtic ancestry of the land.

With such a strong and enduring cultural identity, it is not hard to arrive at the conclusion that, with the Romans only recently arrived in their lands, the Dumnonii of the Boudican period would be hostile towards their unwanted guests and volatile enough to erupt into acts of violence against the occupying Roman forces at any time. This would be particularly true if those resentments and hostilities had been further whipped up by the arrival of Druids, possibly even the same ones who had worked to broker an agreement between Boudica and her allies and were now bringing word to the Dumnonii that the time had come for the tribes to throw off the Roman yoke.

The deeply revered Druids would have been warmly welcomed by any of the tribes of Britain, and not least in the lands of the Dumnonii. Could it then be that having had a hand in plotting the start of the rebellion, the Druids travelled to the lands of the Dumnonii and other tribes in a further attempt to foment unrest and rebellious activity against the Romans? With the seeds of revolt then sown so far afield, the Druids would then be on their way to accomplishing their goal of stretching Roman resources beyond their effective limits and ultimately causing a shock wave which would bring the whole Roman administration of Britain crashing to the ground. How else could the Druids halt the killing machine that was gradually wiping their holy order off the face of Britain? Certainly the Druids on Mona were all dead and their sacred groves lay in ruins, their ashes stamped into the ground by the garrisons that now controlled their sites. But if the Romans could be stopped now, the Druidic order could still be restored and live safely once more in a land that was free of their tormentors. Many of the order could have fled the persecution to the temporary safety of the unoccupied tribal lands or crossed the sea to Ireland, the *insula sacra* of which the Romans never managed to take control. With the Romans gone these once powerful priests could return again to rebuild the order and restore the Celtic culture of Britain.

Whatever the reason, the latest archaeological evidence certainly tends to suggest that Poenius Postumus was caught between a rock and a hard place. His duty was to obey his governor's orders, but he was also committed to maintaining order in the areas under his own command. Neglect of either requirement could spell disaster for the Roman administration, but the choice had to be made. If the reasons for his problems are as suggested, his refusal to send reinforcements probably turned out to be the right choice. Of course, on a personal level his decision proved to be disastrous, but when considered tactically it made sense. If Postumus had been unable to contain his own problems and subsequently lost control of the territory under his command then it could very easily have spelt the end of Roman Britain. Instead, it appears that his decision not only prevented Paulinus from becoming faced with a more widespread rebellion, it also possibly saved his own legion from being overrun and perhaps destroyed due to being below strength.

There is no way of knowing whether or not Postumus ever had the opportunity to get word to Paulinus of the reasons for his decision, but when it was finally over and the governor was back in control of the province, the old soldier did the only thing that a senior Roman officer who had disobeyed his superior's orders could do. Roman honour demanded to be satisfied and Postumus did not shirk from his duty, ending his once glittering career by falling on perhaps the very sword with which he had battled his way up the ranks.

THE XX LEGION MOVES NORTH

If Paulinus was badly let down by the failure of the II Augusta to send him the support he had ordered, he could at least take heart from the fact that the XX Legion had obeyed his rallying call and a vexillation of their legionaries was marching up to join the coming fight.

It has been argued that the XX Legion could not easily have provided the men that Paulinus needed, at this particular point of their service in Britain, without running the risk of using up almost all of their available complement of troops, then operating around the central and southern Welsh border lands. Certain modern commentators have suggested that the legion was still well under strength at the time of the Boudican revolt, and have put forward the argument that its establishment was initially greatly reduced after its veterans were demobbed and settled in the brand new *colonia* at Camulodunum. The remaining complement was further run down when it was seriously mauled by the Silures during the time of Publius Ostorius Scapula's final campaigns in Wales and the start of the governorship of Aulus Didius Gallus in AD 52.

This reasoning seems somewhat flawed, however, when one considers the number and size of the fortifications that were in operational use within the zone where the XX Legion was posted. It is true that the settling veterans were discharged at Camulodunum in AD 49, which is when the XX Legion established its then most westerly base at Kingsholme near Gloucester. Certainly at this juncture the legion would have been under strength, having just pensioned off and settled its veterans, and there is the additional point that the new fortress was only capable of housing a vexillation of some 2,500 men. This goes some way to indicating the strength of the legion at the time it was first posted west. However, the legion could easily have been brought up to strength later with new recruits from overseas, as is the case in Cassius Dio's account of the rebuilding of the IX Hispana's strength after their disastrous encounter with Boudica. After seventeen or so years in occupation the Romans had a well-established and free-flowing system of communication and supply between the ports of the south and east coasts and the units posted to what could be regarded as the front line. This system not only helped to speed up the urbanisation and Romanisation of conquered land but was also vital if the Romans were to continue to maintain support for the units operating in the hostile territories.

In the period running up to the revolt the XX Legion may well have been deployed in a similar manner to II Augusta, which had, as previously explained, been operating in separate detachments for many years before finally re-forming into one body at Isca Dumnoniorum. Supporting this assertion is the fact that the XX Legion very probably also built the base of Burrium, around forty miles south-west of Kingsholme near Usk in Monmouthshire.

This was an ideally placed base from which to conduct operations against the Silures, and was another vexillation-sized fortress constructed whilst the original base at Kingsholme was still operational. Kingsholme probably did not in fact fall out of use until the XX Legion moved to their new headquarters at the legionary fortress of Glevum, built at nearby Gloucester sometime around AD 64 and capable of accommodating the whole unit.

Whilst Tacitus, in book XII of the *Annals*, does make reference to the fact that many Roman troops were lost in the Welsh theatre, he also states that Roman losses were exaggerated by both sides. The Britons inflated their claim, he says, to scare the incoming Governor Aulus Didius Gallus, and Gallus himself is likely to have exaggerated the Roman losses as a way of enhancing any victory he might later win over the Silures. At any rate, heavy losses or not, it seems highly unlikely that the gaps in the legion strength would not have been plugged over the eight or nine years that elapsed between the arrival of Gallus and the start of the Boudican revolt, especially given that war with the tribe was both widespread and vicious in its nature. Scapula had set the tone of the conflict before his death by declaring his intention to wipe out the Silures completely. The tribe, upon learning of this, became enraged at the threat of their intended extermination, and this led to many years of vicious fighting which saw a combination of open battles and guerrilla fighting. Even with the support of auxiliary units it seems doubtful that a legion that was significantly under strength, and was not being reinforced with fresh men, could sustain this type of campaign for long. It would therefore seem more sensible to assume that, on top of a fresh draft to fill the gap left by the veterans, the legion was being replenished during this period by replacements for battlefield losses.

A final piece of evidence for the strength of the XX Legion at the time of the revolt is the vexillation fortress at Clyro in Powys. This seems to have been built somewhere around AD 60 and was perhaps intended to replace an earlier fortress situated a few miles north-east at Clifford. This earlier establishment, although smaller, was capable of housing a garrison of nearly 3,000 legionaries and auxiliary cavalry. There would be little reason for building such large fortresses and keeping them operational in a very active theatre of war if there were insufficient numbers of troops to provide an effective garrison for them. After all, there would be no tactical value in building a fort in hostile territory and then leaving it so poorly defended that it could not be held. As it appears that there are at least three large forts operational around the time of the revolt, we can only form the conclusion that the legion which garrisoned them must have been around full strength in order to man them effectively.

Like II Augusta and IX Hispana, the XX Legion was one of the original legions which took part in the Claudian invasion of AD 43. Originally raised in Pannonia by Tiberius, it was Augustan in origin. At the time of the invasion it was part of the Roman army of the Rhine territories and was based at Novaesium, now Neuss in Germany. In the years prior to the revolt the legion is generally referred to as XX Valeria and a host of possibilities exist as to the origin of this name, ranging from one of the unit's early generals, Valerian, to the highly unlikely suggestion of the adulterous Valeria Messalina, wife of Claudius. It is more likely that the legion carried no titles until after the Boudican revolt, when it was awarded the titles of *Valeria*, referring to its valiant status, and *Victrix* meaning 'victorious'.

It would seem that at the time of the Boudican revolt its commander exhibited none of the reluctance displayed by Poenius Postumus, and readily complied with the order to send troops to assist Paulinus's stand against the rebels. This could be viewed as further evidence that the legion was strong enough to cope with the abstraction of a large body of men and still have sufficient strength to keep the Welsh tribes contained in their own areas. It may also be the case that the legate of the XX Legion had by this time received word that Poenius Postumus was not going to send men, and quickly realised that his was now the only legion other than the XIIII Gemina in a position to provide significant help to Paulinus.

Here was an opportunity for the XX Legion to save the day. Yes, he was under orders, but if glory was to be had then his legion was certainly going to claim its share, and he would send a vexillation of seasoned troops to seize it.

In the early Imperial Roman army the first cohort was the most prestigious unit of the legion. Within its ranks were the senior centurions and the most experienced troops. When the legion marched out of camp, it was the first cohort which marched with the Aquila and Imago standards at its head – powerful symbols which embodied the spirit and pride of the legion and proclaimed the loyalty of the unit to the divine Emperor. Even in its makeup it was different to the other cohorts of the legion. Whereas a normal cohort consisted of six centuries of eighty men, the first cohort reflected the strength of the old Republican maniple and was often made up of five double centuries, taking its nominal strength to 800 men. Governor Paulinus would have had urgent need of the best troops he could gather together, so it is very likely that, of the various cohorts of the XX Legion, the first cohort is the one most likely to have been sent. The additional provision of a further three regular cohorts would have taken the vexillation strength up to 2,240; assuming the legion was up to full strength, that would have left a garrison strength of around 3,000 legionaries and associated staff to maintain a presence in their own areas, not including the various auxiliary units posted to the region.

Marching from their base at Kingsholme, it would have taken the force little more than three days to reach their destination in the heart of the Midlands where they would have met up with Paulinus's army and taken their place in the force that was gathering to do battle with the approaching rebels. Piece by piece, a comparatively small but formidable army group was forming which would soon prove to have a devastating effect on its enemy. At its heart would be an entire battle-hardened legion: the XIIII Gemina.

THE XIIII GEMINA — PAULINUS'S HAMMER

As with II Augusta, the XIIII Gemina Legion adopted the Capricorn as its emblem, thereby indicating that it was raised under Augustus. It was probably formed from an amalgamation of two older legions, hence the 'Gemina' or 'twin' title. This was another of the original four legions which came ashore in AD 43. Having received its orders to move, the XIIII Gemina assembled with the rest of the invasion force after marching to Portus Itius from their base at Mogontiacum on the Rhine, which is now the city of Mainz in Germany.

Of all of the legions that served in Britain at one time or another, the XIIII Gemina is perhaps the least well attested to, given a distinct lack of solid evidence for the movements of the legion. This includes a rarity of monumental inscriptions and other finds, which normally bear out the presence of a certain unit in any particular geographical area. However, whilst a lack of archaeological evidence frustrates our knowledge of the movement of the legion in Britain, Tacitus helpfully makes direct reference to their presence at the final battle with Boudica, which leaves no doubt as to what part the legion played in ending the Boudican revolt.

Following on the heels of Paulinus, the XIIII Gemina, plus an attendant force of auxiliary cavalry and infantry, would have left the devastated Druid stronghold of Mona, marched across the top of North Wales and back into Cheshire. Here they would have followed the line of Watling Street and crossed the River Dee at what is now Chester, where the largest of the legionary fortresses of Britain was later built. This fortress was eventually to become a site covering over twenty-five hectares and was initially occupied by the II Legion Adiutrix Pia Fidelis, before being taken over by the XX Legion Valeria Victrix upon their return from Scotland. Prior to this, at the time the XIIII Gemina passed through, the area was probably the location of a large campaign camp built to house the legion as it conducted its operations in Wales.

Having crossed Cheshire the legion battle group would then have entered what is now Shropshire and bypassed their first permanent home at the fortress of Viroconium Cornoviorum at Wroxeter on the Shropshire Plain. They would then have pressed on into Staffordshire and, as archaeological evidence suggests, possibly stopped off at Pennocrucium near to the village of Water Eaton, before reaching Letocetum, now the village of Wall. Originally Letocetum was home to a large contingent of the XIIII Gemina before the legion moved west to Wroxeter, but evidence suggests that the area also served as the site of a temporary camp during the march back down Watling Street. An examination of the map of Roman roads in Britain also seems to indicate that the area would have been an ideal place for the legion to rendezvous with the column sent up from Kingsholme. The troops would then have had just a short march to complete before they arrived at Manduessedum, now Mancetter, next to the small market town of Atherstone in north Warwickshire.

In the early years of the Roman invasion, the site at Manduessedum was probably occupied by a campaign fort of the XIIII Gemina to maintain control along the Fosse Way, the line of which was then the border between occupied and unconquered territory. Later a much bigger fortress was built there which covered an area of roughly twenty-five hectares. Over the years the fortress at Mancetter has been the subject of much debate concerning both its purpose and its date of construction. The site lies on a low rise above the western bank of the River Anker, overlooking the flood plain and facing east. This naturally leads us to the conclusion that whatever threat it was built to counter was likely to have come from the east, exactly the direction that the Boudican forces would appear from if they ventured that far west.

Archaeological evaluation of Roman Mancetter was carried out for many years by the late Keith Scott, who did much to improve understanding of the site itself. Some of the more recent work carried out by Mr Scott tends to indicate that the fort may well have been in use at the time of the rebellion. If the army of Paulinus did

occupy the site, an explanation of its role relative to the revolt now
needs to be presented.

THE UNHOLY FIRE

For now we will ignore the popular assertion that Mancetter was
indeed the site of the final battle between Paulinus and Boudica.
Instead we shall turn to the possible explanation that rather than
being a battlefield, the site was the place where the Roman forces
congregated, using the fortress both as a staging point for units ready
to go into battle and as a centre of operations from which to launch
a series of raids on the local populace. These raids would have been
specifically devised to provoke the rebels to advance on the precise
area where Paulinus felt confident enough to take them on in open
battle. By necessity, this was something that Paulinus would have
needed to bring about as quickly as possible, because although his
choice of ground was made, time was a luxury he did not have on
his side.

By now Boudica and her rebels would have been creeping
steadily northwards across country, perhaps closing on their next
suggested objective of Ratae Coritanorum. However, although the
rebel force was moving roughly in the direction that best suited the
strategy Paulinus had in mind, their progress may not have been
as swift as he would have wished. As the rebel host grew bigger,
swelled not only with those willing to fight but also with growing
number of non-combatants, the march north would have got
slower and slower, especially as the active elements made good use
of their passage through unprotected territory and set upon every
household, outpost and settlement they encountered along the way.
Such a delay in joining battle may have strengthened the rebels'
hand, but for Paulinus it posed a serious problem. With the Boudican
army dominating the ground further south and war with the Welsh
tribes ongoing in the west, there would be no chance of re-supply

from either of those parts of the country; in order to sustain his force he would therefore have to rely on the supply reserves of the nearby garrisons of the Midlands, which would cause even more logistical problems if the situation was allowed to continue. With all of his available men gathered and preparations for the battle in hand, Paulinus would need to draw the rebels up country quickly so as to provoke a decisive engagement and settle the matter one way or the other.

In order to facilitate this, Paulinus would now need to goad Boudica's army into reacting sufficiently violently for the rebels to speed up their northward advance and then turn west, thereby engaging him on his chosen ground. For that to happen he would also need to enrage them to such a degree that Boudica and her lieutenants, even if they were able to stay focused enough on their prime objective, would be virtually powerless to keep the assembled tribal factions on course for Ratae and would ultimately find themselves forced to go with the wishes of the mob as they turned for the waiting Romans.

Long before the arrival of the Romans in Warwickshire, the countryside around Manduessedum was probably dotted with sites which held a special sacred significance to the native Britons. Even the name Manduessedum is thought to be a Latinised version of a British name meaning 'the place of the chariots'. Whilst some have suggested that this name may indicate that the battle did perhaps take place there, it is probably more likely to be indicative of its origins as an area of some significance to the local ancient tribal population, perhaps as an important meeting place.

Having first established a sizeable military base at Manduessedum, the Romans later significantly downgraded the size of their garrison, and the area was gradually given over to civilian industrial activities such as pottery production and metal working; however, these activities did not begin to flourish in the area until after the time of the revolt. At this time, other than the presence of the fortress and a small associated civilian presence, Manduessedum would have had little to speak of in the way of a larger established settlement. The wider area would still have comprised the small scattered communities typical of Coritanian population distribution. Along with their various sites of worship, these small rural settlements would have been perfect targets with which to provoke a response from the rebel horde.

While the bulk of Paulinus's force made ready for battle, fast-moving cavalry parties could have ridden out from their holding areas and ravaged the countryside with fire and sword. The ancient sacred groves would have gone the way of those on Mona, totally devastated as the Roman raiding parties sought them out and destroyed them one by one, hacking the trees down and torching the groves. The native civilian population would also be fair game now as, under direct orders from their commander, the soldiers attacked the settlements and set about terrorising the populace. Nobody would have been left untouched by the brutality of the troops as they torched homesteads and set about the residents, murdering, looting and raping. Just as the rebels had done to Roman towns before them, the soldiers would have executed their task with brutal efficiency, with neither age nor sex posing a barrier to the torment that they brought with them. This was their chance to pay back the rebels for the slaughter they had carried out in the attacked towns; this was their brand of justice.

In our modern world it is sometimes easy for us to look back at the ancient world and regard such victimisation of the civilian populace with a degree of scepticism or disbelief. We would prefer to look at it as an exaggeration of the ability of the ancient people to kill their fellows so freely. However, the unpleasant truth of the matter is that the ability to kill the innocent indiscriminately is still within us today, only covered over by the very thin veneer of the supposed higher evolution of our cultures. Today, our so-called civilised sensibilities are continually offended by the atrocities and horrors of our own world. Modern military-backed powers the world over, legitimate or otherwise, have perpetuated state terrorism. They have sown vast fields of anti-personnel mines which kill and maim thousands of innocents every year. People's homes are bulldozed into the ground because they oppose their governments' policies and thousands have been wiped off the face of the earth, ethnically cleansed for having a different culture and beliefs. All of this and more has been carried out under the orders of an individual or organisation purporting to act in the interests of their state. With that willingness of man to carry out such acts still very much alive and well today, it is not so hard for us to be able to accept that two millennia ago, in a far more vicious, violent and brutal world, soldiers of one of the original superpowers were eminently capable of unthinkingly carrying out their orders and performing callous acts of murder and inhumanity in the service of the state.

Our complex system of values makes it possible for modern Western society to turn a blind eye to the unsavoury acts that have been carried out on its behalf, and yet stand in moral indignation at other countries which, to a greater or lesser degree, carry out essentially the same kind of acts to achieve their own agenda. Two thousand years ago, while the higher echelons of Roman society may have exercised such double standards, the soldiers of Paulinus's army did not operate under the same code and the motivations for their actions were much simpler. The troops had been in Britain for a long time and had spent many years fighting the various tribes. Through years of fighting and killing they would have become largely desensitised to the horrors of war.

Today, developing technology has helped to sanitise warfare and transform it into a more long-distance affair. Less reliance on personnel and ever more reliance on automated weapons systems mean that the very character of the battlefield has changed drastically. The worst of today's battlefields would have difficulty coming anywhere close to the slaughterhouse environment of an ancient battlefield as opposing armies stood face to face and hacked, stabbed and bludgeoned each other to death. In addition, death, in its many forms, was of far greater influence to ancient people than it is today. Whereas now we generally prefer not to look at death too closely, in the ancient world it was there for everybody to see. In ritual, in justice, in everyday life and even in entertainment, death was all around. In today's world the vast majority of people would regard the immediate sight or presence of a corpse as stressful and shocking and choose, by and large, to avoid all close contact with the dead. Unlike the people of today, ancient society could not choose to avoid death as its shadow was a constant presence in their lives.

To the Roman soldiers let loose on the local people, the brutality they would have used upon the terrified civilians had become just a commonplace part of their lives. They had no connection or loyalty to these people, many of them did not even have the same ethnic heritage as the Britons, and, as Tacitus has suggested, the local population was now freely displaying its contempt for Paulinus and his troops; the people now needed little encouragement to vent their hostility on the Romans when they thought their own deliverance was at hand. The Roman soldiers, angered by the open displays of hostility and hardened to the horrors of war, would also need little encouragement. Far away from home, with no connection to these people and eager to avenge the rebel victories, it would be a very easy thing for the ordinary Roman soldier to carry out any instruction to attack the local civilians without giving it a second thought.

As the soldiers carried out their orders, and the roundhouses and sacred groves burned, Paulinus would have been confident that his men would follow his orders to the letter and that a number of the local civilians would be deliberately spared, surviving the campaign of terror to become unwitting bait in a trap that he had carefully laid. He would have known that some of those survivors would be sending word to Boudica and the rebels as soon as they could, telling the rebel army of the atrocities that were being carried out on peaceful folk who had no part in the rebellion and begging the rebels to come and save their homes. Buoyed up by the success of their seemingly unstoppable advance and spoiling now for the next great fight, once word spread through the rebel army that the Romans were killing and persecuting innocent peasants, Paulinus knew they would come to him.

7

THE BATTLE

Perhaps the most widely accepted suggestion for the location of the last battle between Boudica and the Roman forces under the command of Governor Paulinus is the wide expanse of land next to the site of the vexillation fortress at Mancetter, then known as Manduessedum. Although it is at first very tempting to accept that the area could be the lost battlefield, the site quickly begins to lose its viability when it is placed under closer scrutiny.

Anyone wishing to form a convincing theory as to where the battlefield is located will first need to refer to the sparse documentary evidence available. The chief clue to the site of the battle is held in the one known description of the ground that survives, in Tacitus's *Annals*. Far from mentioning the many crucial features that Paulinus would have taken into account when choosing a site, Tacitus gives us only the vaguest snapshot of what the site may have looked like:

> He chose a position in a defile with a wood behind him. There could then be, he knew, no enemy, except at his front where lay open country with no cover for ambushes.
>
> (Tacitus, *Annals* XIV.34)

As if this almost complete lack of information was not bad enough, the problems in pinning down the location of the site are further compounded by the emergence of certain slight variations when Tacitus's Latin text is rendered into English by different modern translators. Furthermore, even though the tiny passage in Tacitus is the only near-contemporary description of the site, it is not an eyewitness account but was written years later from at least second-hand sources of information. Any attempt to indicate the location of the field solely on the basis of this description therefore stands a very real chance of proving to be inaccurate. The possibility of a mistake becomes especially likely when closer attention is paid to the many tactical considerations that Paulinus would have needed to make when choosing his ground, as this is where the suggestion for the site being at Mancetter begins to fall apart.

Perhaps the most important element on which to focus in Tacitus's sketchy description of the battlefield is the word 'defile', since most theories on the location of the site depend upon isolating a feature within the topography of the proposed area that fits this key descriptive component. When used in a topographical context, the word is always defined by English dictionaries as a narrow pass, valley or gorge. In its strictest sense, this is a feature in which the site at Mancetter is once more found wanting.

In laying out his proposal for the site at Mancetter, the late Dr Graham Webster indicated that the Roman army might have taken up position in a narrow gorge facing north-east, backed by wooded slopes and located just to the south of the site of the vexillation fortress. In this respect the area does indeed correspond to the classical description in as much as the gorge faces out over an open and relatively flat plain, something that fits in well with the mention of the enemy being denied cover for ambushes. However, the problems with the site become much more evident when one considers more carefully the natural features within the proposed area in which the Roman troops would be formed up prior to their going into battle against the rebel army.

The first point to consider is that, if this was the actual position chosen by Paulinus, the Roman formation would have been very tightly packed into the confines of the gorge. The proposed area identified by Webster for the location of the Roman force would involve around 10,000 men, including roughly 1,000 cavalry, occupying an area of around half a kilometre square. They would be further disadvantaged by being hemmed in at the rear and on two sides by steep and heavily wooded slopes that at certain points rise in excess of fifty metres above the plain. Whilst Tacitus does mention this point and declares it to be an advantage, these supposed tactical benefits are apparently not supported in the version supplied by Cassius Dio:

> Paulinus could not extend his line the whole length of hers, because, even if the troops had been drawn up only one deep, they would not have reached far enough, because they were so inferior in their numbers; nor, on the other hand, did he dare join battle in a single compact force, for fear of being surrounded and cut to pieces. He therefore divided his army into three divisions, in order to fight at several points at once, and he made each of the divisions so strong that it could not easily be broken through.
>
> (Cassius Dio, *Roman Histories* LXII.8)

Whilst Dio echoes a later part of Tacitus's account when he mentions that the Roman force was broken up into three divisions, he also states that the soldiers were not confined to one dense formation, something which makes great tactical sense given the fact that, were the Roman troops actually to have been positioned within the narrow gorge, they would indeed have been grouped into one large mass and would subsequently have been very short of space to manoeuvre. This would not only have made movement of individual formations difficult, it would also have meant that any deployment of the various individual units would have been greatly hindered by the close proximity of neighbouring units which were themselves trying to form up into their own battle positions. With a vast force of Britons approaching their front, it would also have been foolhardy for Paulinus to have placed his men in a position where they had no chance of withdrawing and regrouping.

In addition, it seems inconceivable that the Roman army would ever deliberately place itself in a position where it would be denied the opportunity to fully employ the formation tactics which had won it victory on so many previous occasions. The deployment of such manoeuvres would be vital if they were going to succeed against an opponent easily capable of quickly surrounding them and engulfing the entire force if it was allowed to do so.

Crucially, in the position that Webster suggests, the entire Roman formation would only ever have been able to pull back into the gorge. Here their retreat would have been cut off by the steep and possibly heavily wooded slopes that stood to the rear and sides. Trapped at this point, their only option would be to make a last desperate stand and inevitably be crushed by the onrush of the much bigger opposing force. The enemy would no doubt by then have seized the upper hand by pushing home a mass charge after seeing their opponents making a withdrawal. Once this had happened, and the Roman forces were in retreat, the chances of regrouping before the defile and recovering any sort of advantage would have been nigh on impossible to achieve. The speed of the Britons' pursuit would allow them to stream around the Roman flanks and, from the front, roll over any attempt to stop and hold ground. Paulinus would then not only have lost any chance of saving Roman control of the province, he would also have committed the grave tactical errors of deliberately cutting off his own line of retreat and failing to put into place an adequate backup plan if things did not go his way.

Fully aware as he was of being outnumbered and in a potentially grave situation, it seems very unlikely that a general of Paulinus's calibre and experience would have made such apparently basic and terminal errors.

On a much more simple level, the topography of the area around Mancetter would have posed further problems for the Roman troops in that the direction from which the enemy was coming would have meant Paulinus's troops would be going into battle on an often marshy flood plain. Additionally they would have to contend with a low uphill gradient over much of their advance, which is likely to have made a significant reduction in the impetus of their final charge into battle. As they were so heavily outnumbered, Paulinus would have wanted an area where his formations could have operated to maximum effect. As it was, with the slight slope falling towards him and his men penned in by the enclosing gorge, any British onrush would be devastating if his men could not clear the gorge; they would find themselves unable to implement their normal tactics and would be overrun and hacked to pieces by a dense and unstoppable wave of rebels.

Finally, the existence of one natural feature in particular would have marked the area out as totally unsuitable for such a crucial engagement. The River Anker winds its way directly through the proposed site, about a kilometre to the east of the proposed Roman lines. Although not what one would consider a large water course, the river would have posed enough of an obstacle to be capable of badly disrupting the cohesion of the rapidly advancing Roman formations. The infantry would not only have to contend with sustaining a charge while wading through water up to waist height and carrying full armour and equipment, they would then have to deal with the problem of keeping their footing on the river bed. The banks would have become extremely slippery after the first of their comrades had made the crossing; if any of the soldiers stumbled or went under it would no doubt have had a serious knock-on effect on the men following. This might have badly disrupted the order of the formations and thereby created an unwanted delay while the formations were once more re-formed as they emerged on the opposite bank.

The impact of ordered, efficiently working formations was going to be crucial if the Romans were to be successful in their efforts against the Boudican force. Paulinus would clearly be jeopardising all of this if he decided to take a gamble and risk the crossing of the Anker during his advance. In the final analysis, with so much potential for disaster, the site at Mancetter could never have been an option for Paulinus, given that it offered hardly anything that would help to ensure a successful outcome for the Roman force.

As the Mancetter area now appears to be an unlikely one for staging such a crucial engagement, the question that now begs an answer is: if not Mancetter, then where?

Choosing the correct ground to host a battle which was going to be nothing short of a make-or-break encounter was going to be crucial – especially with regard to the continued Roman occupation of Britain. Paulinus would have therefore needed to put as many ticks in boxes as he possibly could when he set about determining the suitability of a particular site.

From a broader perspective, by choosing a site in the central Midlands, Paulinus could put distance between himself and the Boudican rebels, who were now moving northwards towards their next objective. Because he had left his main force awaiting his return, and since the rebel force would be moving relatively slowly compared to the speed of typical Roman marching columns, Paulinus would now be in a position to use both time and his encamped men to make preparations for the coming battle. He would have no need to move any further south as his enemy would eventually arrive in the general area, and when he felt ready he could provoke them into being drawn in and launching an attack on his force. This would mean that he could start the engagement on his own terms, able to dictate both the location of the battle and the timing of it.

As if to further dispel the suggestion that the battle was actually fought further south, it is worth considering the view that there would be no point in him marching his troops any further down Watling Street to engage the rebels. Doing this would only reduce opportunities for choosing and preparing a suitable site; it would also take him further away from a much safer area, one where he would be most quickly able to draw on the reserves of the many garrisons that were dotted around the central, north and western Midlands. These garrisons held troops that would be vital to any backup plan he may have formulated in the event that the worst-case scenario did happen and the Romans were defeated in the next big engagement with the rebels.

Paulinus's final choice of ground, therefore, would in the first instance need to be a site within the same general area as Mancetter, allowing him to capitalise on that nearby support. Secondly, it had to be an area which would offer his army every possible topographical advantage while also denying the enemy any significant chance of making capital from the location. In searching for a possible site today, the area that seems most likely to fit all of those requirements is the site once known as Venonis.

THE CASE FOR VENONIS

Situated on the border of Warwickshire and Leicestershire, Venonis – known today as High Cross – sits on the top of a large rise in the land and overlooks an expansive panorama encompassing many square miles of typical English farmland. High Cross lies where a rural stretch of the B4455 meets the busy A5. This intersection of two modern roads is also the only visible physical clue that the location is also the site of an extremely important Roman road junction, where the great arterial routes of the Fosse Way and Watling Street once crossed and formed the very hub of the Roman military road system. Today a good deal of heavy traffic thunders along Watling Street, with a variety of private and commercial vehicles still capitalising on the direct route cutting across the country that the legions created nearly 2,000 years ago. The Warwickshire section of the Fosse Way, however, now much reduced in status, offers a peaceful, tree-lined leisure drive, passing quiet rural communities on a route that moves up the length of the country in a north-easterly direction towards its terminus at High Cross. At this point the Fosse Way ceases quite abruptly to remain a useable road and disappears under the Leicestershire countryside, not surfacing again until it once more rejoins the modern road system and links up with the B4114 near the village of Sutton in the Elms. Here it resumes its typically Roman, arrow-straight course and heads straight into the heart of Leicester, the ancient Roman *civitas* of Ratae Coritanorum, before heading off towards the city of Lincoln.

Taking up a position on the top of High Cross and looking in a roughly easterly direction, it is easy to observe the straight line of Watling Street as it makes its way off for some miles into the distance. One is also immediately struck by the way the land gently falls away in a steady downward gradient over a distance of around a mile and in a broadly sweeping arc. If one turns around to look north-west along the route of Watling Street one can again observe the course of the road dipping down and briefly disappearing from view as it cuts through, and then surfaces from, the area known as Smockington Hollow, the lowest point of which is around another mile in that direction. Lying close to the bottom of the hollow is the old Wigston Parva fort, a semi-permanent Roman fort whose existence was first discovered in the late 1960s. Limited excavations have been carried out at the site, and it is believed that the fort was active during the Claudian period and housed a garrison of auxiliary troops before being dismantled. It was probably built to serve as a frontier post prior to the Romans pushing west beyond the old occupation border of the Fosse Way. The site is the only known Roman fortification with any degree of permanence lying within the immediate area of the settlement of Venonis.

At the time of the Boudican revolt there would apparently have been very little to see at Venonis. It may be that it existed as a minor military outpost, perhaps a small way-station to accommodate the coming and goings of military couriers and the like, but the beginnings of a permanent settlement on the site do not seem to have taken place until a few years after the end of the revolt. Once the site was properly established it seems to have prospered well enough, benefiting both from its position on the junction of the main roads and the protection of its own purpose-built perimeter defence works. Archaeological investigation of the site and its environs indicates that Venonis was active right up to the end of the fourth century and was the focus for a small scattering of private villas built within sight of it, suggesting that the post-Boudican phases were reasonably prosperous times for the residents of the area.

At first glance there would appear to be nothing within the area to indicate that this could be the site of the battlefield. No archaeological evidence has yet been uncovered from prior to the establishment of the civilian settlement which might suggest either the presence of a large Roman force or its involvement in a large-scale engagement in the immediate area with Boudica's rebel army. In addition there is also the need to address the most important of the clues mentioned by Tacitus, and quantify the existence of the defile relative to the area.

While it is not easily possible to verify that, 2,000 years ago, the dense areas of woodland mentioned by Tacitus could be found lying to the west of High Cross, it is easier to table the argument that Venonis could be the area of the defile mentioned in Tacitus's account of the battle. If one is prepared to move away from the common preconception that lingers from earlier proposals – that the mouth of the said feature opened up to face the advancing enemy – then a more flexible approach can be adopted when considering the available possibilities.

If Paulinus had selected Venonis as the site of the battle then the ground would have been ideal for his greatly outnumbered force to attempt a stand against an enemy that was, numerically at least, much more powerful than his own. The presence of Smockington Hollow to the rear of the ground would be of greater benefit to him than any gorge opening up to face his foe. Rather than being confined by the limitations of a head-on orientation, Smockington Hollow actually runs almost parallel to the ground most suitable for engaging the rebel army. This would mean that he could ready his men in formation just east of the point where the ground falls away into the hollow, thereby affording his men the protection of the defile prior to their advancing. It would also mean that Paulinus could keep a sizeable chunk of his formation out of plain sight until he was ready to send them into battle. Their appearance on the head of the rise would serve as an unwelcome surprise to the advancing Britons, who would no doubt be thinking that they were in for an easy fight, about to slaughter a much smaller force of Romans than the one which had now appeared on the ground ahead.

With Smockington Hollow at his back, Paulinus's position would be extremely difficult to assault without inviting heavy losses. Since the defile covered the rear of the Roman battle lines, the only way to reach the troops positioned on the top of High Cross, from any direction, would be to rush the lines in an uphill head-on charge. This would have quickly sapped the strength of those involved and reduced the impetus of any advance, to the great detriment to Boudica's force, given that charging infantry are always less effective when pushing uphill. In choosing High Cross, therefore, Paulinus would have secured every advantage: not only would he have been in a position where he could confidently begin his own advance and then launch subsequent charges downhill, he would also be dominating the ground on the vital road junction of Watling Street and the Fosse Way. This location offered the prospect both of carrying extra troops to his position and providing possible lines of retreat if things began to swing in the Britons' favour.

If the chance of further reinforcements seems remote, it is worth considering that a general as experienced as Paulinus would have tried to capitalise on every advantage he could muster. We cannot know if he still held any sort of hope of receiving aid from the II Augusta, or even from the troops under the command of Cerialis further north; however, it certainly makes sense that he would take up a position where, if help was on its way, it would reach him as quickly as possible. There would be no better place for this to happen than on the junction of the two most important roads in the province.

THE ARCHAEOLOGY OF HIGH CROSS

Today, when one looks out from the top of High Cross, there is little to see by way of permanent human habitation. Large expanses of farmland sweep away in all directions, dotted here and there by small collections of farm buildings, whose occupants put the rolling fields to a variety of uses such as dairy farming, wool production and the cultivation of cereals and other bulk crops. There is the odd little village or tiny hamlet of the kind that one tends to come across, almost by surprise, if one decides to leave the hectic A5 and take a leisurely drive through the quiet country lanes that meander through the countryside. There is very little to indicate to the casual observer that the area ever had any significant phases of occupation other than the rural peace and quiet that it currently enjoys. However, a more detailed look at the site reveals a reasonably continuous history of occupancy. The timeline of occupation runs from back beyond the Neolithic and Bronze Age, on into the Iron Age and the Roman period and then onwards into the post-Roman era before revealing evidence of later occupation in the medieval period and so into modern times.

Perhaps the most striking visual evidence of one of its previous phases can be seen from the air directly above the area of the ancient road junction. Here the extent of the Roman settlement of Venonis is dramatically outlined. Clearly visible lines indicate the northern corner of its former defences. Largely invisible on the ground, the lines of the ditches and earthworks that once protected the Roman civilian community stand out in bold relief when they are viewed from high up in the air. However, the advantages of such a perfect bird's eye view are not limited to allowing one to define the ghostly imprint of the once significant settlement. Many more clues that point to possible Roman military activity at the site begin to surface when the immediate area around the former civilian settlement is more closely examined.

Although largely unexplored or inconclusively interpreted by archaeologists at present, clear marks and features are visible within the landscape of High Cross which may suggest that Roman forces not only made temporary camps in the area but also carried out some type of engineering work. This may lead one to conclude that the ground around the top of the rise had been deliberately fortified, perhaps to prepare the site for battle. Furthermore, it appears that those particular features do not appear to be related in any way to the settlement of Venonis.

One of the undated and as yet unclassified features within the area of High Cross is a low earthwork to the immediate north of the site. This follows a course from west to east across open fields, travelling at its closest point some 100 metres north of the building complex which now occupies the piece of land closest to the modern road junction, very close to the centre of what was once Venonis. The feature is some 500 metres long and appears to consist of up to two parallel banks and ditches. Given its position and length, it is doubtful that the earthwork has anything to do with the defences of the civilian site. However, due to its obvious characteristics it does seem as though the feature was constructed with some sort of defensive purpose in mind. If that is indeed the case, what was it built to defend?

It would not be unrealistic to suggest that, having chosen the high ground on the junction, Paulinus subsequently felt that the position needed more in the way of defensive qualities. A physical barrier covering this flank could serve to channel the enemy to him from the direction from which he wanted them to approach. His force would have been far too small to be able to deal with an attack from either of the flanks as well as from the front, so the construction of a barrier to protect his force would have been a sensible measure to implement. It was also an easily achievable construction that the Roman army had made good use of in past engagements.

Having then identified that there was no woodland or natural barrier present which he could enhance to perform this task, Paulinus would have started from scratch and set about making his own preparations by tasking his men to dig a shallow ditch along the length of the flank. They would then pile up the spoil that was extracted from the excavations to construct a low earth bank. This earth bank could be topped with a threatening row of sharpened timber stakes, onto which any attackers who were successful at crossing the ditch line would have to throw themselves in order to press home an attack on the defending Romans. Paulinus would no doubt intend that the rebel army, upon seeing the line of the ditch and bank running along his left flank, would recognise the complications of launching any attacks to that area of the Roman lines and instead take the more direct route for a head-on assault, relying on sheer weight of numbers to smash the waiting Roman battle line.

As yet there is no evidence that a structure of this type existed over on what would have been Paulinus's right flank. However, if Paulinus did not build a similar defence work on that flank it could be that no preparation was needed, possibly due to the fact that certain natural defences were already present. It is therefore a very real possibility that the thick woodland mentioned by Tacitus formed a natural barrier that would have offered his force the protection to its right flank that it would have needed.

In addition to the aforementioned fortlet at Wigston Parva, there are two other sites within the area of High Cross which may further indicate the temporary presence of the Roman military.

These sites feature rectilinear crop marks which are very suggestive of the presence of Roman marching camps, a comparatively rare phenomenon in that part of the Midlands. Their regular rectangular shape with rounded corners is typical of the ground plan of such camps, and when examined carefully they do not appear to show any of the tell-tale features of more permanent sites, such as any sign of gate structures in the outer defences. One of these sites is located to the west of High Cross, close to the line of the A5. Although little information is available about this feature, by comparing its size to surrounding features it appears that the site may have been big enough to support a unit around the size of a cohort of up to 500 troops.

The second site is located to the north of High Cross, in the area where a natural spring rises. This is obviously something which the Roman surveyors responsible for siting camps would have been keen to locate, given that it offered a ready supply of clean water for the troops using the camp. Its size and shape is again indicative of a Roman military camp, and the size of the main feature would once more suggest that it was capable of housing around a cohort of troops. Furthermore, there appears to be nothing within its plan which indicates a more permanent purpose. Like the first camp mentioned, it is located in an ideal position close to the road system and out of sight of any force advancing from the east. This second camp differs, however, in the fact that here there appears to be additional evidence of similar types of defences within its own lines, suggesting that the site was used at least twice or more for the same purpose.

In addition to these two possible marching camps, there is also some evidence for a third enclosure of a very similar pattern close to the top of High Cross. However, the visible evidence that would allow an attempt to identify the purpose of the site is here far more vague than the much clearer features of the first two.

If any subsequent archaeological investigations reveal that these features were in fact temporary Roman camps, their presence around the High Cross site, although very interesting, would not in themselves be cast iron proof that any kind of engagement ever took place within the area. In known terms relative to the Roman period, the site represents not only a former settlement but also the junction of two great Roman roads. It would therefore have been a convenient site for Roman military columns that were moving for long distances on the road system to use as a stopping-off point before moving on to their ultimate destinations. Here, in the times after the establishment of the more permanent settlement, the soldiers could rest, re-supply and indulge in a little leisure time while camped outside the settlement.

What makes the camps more interesting regarding their use in a possible battlefield context is their as yet speculative relationship to the presence of the previously mentioned earthwork, and the obvious tactical advantage to the Romans of using High Cross as a battle site. Although it is unlikely that Paulinus would have encamped his entire force around the area on which the battle was to be fought, it seems a perfectly sensible suggestion that, while the main body of his force remained in a holding position at Manduessedum, an advance party made camp at High Cross and began to prepare the site for the coming battle by laying defences and manning a signal post on the summit. These men would effectively have acted somewhat in the capacity of a modern engineer unit. They would have worked on preparations for the arrival of the main force and maintained a watch, waiting for the signal that would travel up Watling Street to tell them that the Boudican force was turning for them. Once seen, the signal would be relayed west and then, just half a day's easy march away, the main force would then be mobilised to make its way to their final positions.

HIGH CROSS — THE ARMIES MEET

Charged by their dramatic run of victories against the hated, alien establishment of Rome, and infuriated by the atrocities that Paulinus was now carrying out on the peaceful communities of the Coritani, the massed army of rebellious Britons decided that now was the time to squash the last of the life out of the army that had oppressed their peoples for so long. There would be no need to take Ratae and enlist the support of the exiled Coritanian chiefs; the Romans were few and they were many. United now, the tribes were ready to take back their lands, and the only thing that stood in their way was a vastly inferior Roman force waiting, so they believed, to be utterly destroyed by their irresistible advance.

No doubt one of the carefully placed Roman signal stations that were located along Watling Street would have spotted the great horde first, appearing on the horizon as it swung west and began to lumber slowly over the countryside towards the final, fateful encounter with the forces of the Roman administration. Any hopes that Boudica and her lieutenants still had about exercising any form of control and staying focused on the next objective were gone as Paulinus's plan started to take hold. Now the rebel leaders would either have to split the great army or be forced to go with the wishes of the majority, to seek the Romans out and smash them before yet more sacred sites were violated and more innocents suffered. Boudica knew that victory could only be achieved if they stayed together, so reluctantly she acceded to their wishes and threw her lot in with those turning west.

It is difficult to imagine what the handful of soldiers at the first signal station must have thought as they first set eyes on the huge, slowly moving swarm of Britons as it rolled over the countryside in an all-enveloping flood. It is doubtful if any of them had ever set eyes on such a massive collection of people before. Their shock and excitement must surely have been evident in the way that instructions were hurriedly and excitedly shouted out. No doubt they would have been liberally punctuated with suitable soldierly oaths and profanities as they set about lighting the beacon that would quickly send the news many miles back up Watling Street to where Paulinus waited. Just to be sure there was going to be no halt in the advance, they would have remained in their positions until the very last minute, before mounting their horses and riding to safety to avoid being engulfed and destroyed by the advancing Britons.

As the quickest and most reliable method of conveying the news, beacon fires placed at intervals along Watling Street would have ensured that the news of Boudica's advance would have travelled quickly and efficiently, either by day or night. The news would have travelled fast between the various signal posts, ensuring that Paulinus would have ample time to mobilise his men and set them out on the short march from Manduessedum to the battlefield he had prepared at High Cross.

With his men already in a high state of readiness, a vast marching column that could have stretched for over two miles in length would have rapidly formed up outside the camps and then made ready to move out onto Watling Street and march the few miles south-east to High Cross. With their prayers and devotions to personal and unit deities now offered, the soldiers would be answering the roll call of the centurions and optios who were now accounting for every man under their command. All of the assembled troops would have been roused that same morning by the daily shout of: *'bellona parate?'* – 'are you ready for war?' Three times they would have roared back: *'parate!'* – 'ready!'

Now, with their wills drawn up and individual collections of coins that represented their savings safely buried in secret spots somewhere near to camp, the soldiers marched out onto Watling Street. Singing the familiar old marching songs and shouting out the war chants and cries that would lift their spirits, they would no doubt be hoping to all the gods that they would soon return in one piece to reclaim their coins and hopefully celebrate a great victory. In the vast column there would not be one soldier who did not know what awaited him at the other end of the march. Word of the size of the rebel army would have returned with a steady stream of the legion's mounted scouts and despatch riders, who would regularly be relaying confirmation of the enemy's strength and disposition to their commander. Still, with the cult of discipline burned deep into their consciousness and, for many, the hardening experience of years of savage warfare against the Britons under their belts, they marched out for what many of them must have thought was probably going to be the last time.

Marching in the great column towards the battlefield would not only be the heavily armoured legionaries of the XIIII Gemina and the XX Legion, but also the various auxiliary infantry and cavalry units that would play a crucial part in the battle. Paulinus would be dependent on the skills and abilities of these men in supporting the efforts of the heavy infantry; without them the day would almost certainly be lost.

Though none of the auxiliary units are actually named in either of the accounts of the battle, it is possible, from a few small clues in the classical accounts and from what is known about the units present in Britain at the time, at least to make some acceptable suggestions as to the identity of these units. For instance, in Tacitus's account of the attack on Mona, he refers to auxiliary troops crossing deep waters by swimming beside their horses. Perhaps the troops most identifiable from the use of this tactic is the Batavian Cohorts. These warriors, who hailed from an area now in the eastern Netherlands, were skilled horsemen and excellent swimmers. They first arrived in Britain with the Claudian invasion force and probably numbered around 4,000, made up of eight part-mounted cohorts, or *cohortes equitatae*, of 500 men apiece. Their skill and prowess during the opening campaigns for the conquest of Britain was first mentioned in Cassius Dio's account of the Battle of the Medway. Believing themselves safe on the other side of the river from the main Roman force, the Britons suddenly found themselves under attack from their flank by the Batavians who, as the only auxiliaries in this theatre of war who specialised in such perilous amphibious crossings, had forded the fast-moving river in full armour and launched a devastating attack on the unsuspecting natives. Their unique ability therefore appears to identify them as the units to which Tacitus refers as crossing the Menai Strait, and thus the soldiers most likely to have joined the march back east to confront the rebel forces.

Two other units could have provided a cavalry presence on the battlefield, as they are known to have been stationed in or around the Midlands at the time. Both the Ala Gallorum Indiana and Ala Primae Pannoniorum probably arrived with the original invasion force and both were quingenary units, 500 strong. Interestingly, the Pannonians also carried the title 'Victrix', the same title that was awarded to both of the participating legions for their role in defeating the rebels.

With a legion and a half, numbering nearly 8,000 men, as the bulwark of his force, Paulinus would then probably have used 1,000 auxiliary infantry and 1,000 cavalry to strengthen the flanks of his battle line and sweep round the sides of the Boudican host. With their armour and kit polished up to create maximum visual impact on their enemies, the site and sound of the column on the march must have been awesome as they made their way along Watling Street. In an easy march over relatively flat terrain, the great column would have taken less than half a day to reach the forming-up point at High Cross, where the various units would have made for their allotted positions in the pre-prepared battle lines ready for a final briefing from the unit commanders. By arriving well in advance of the enemy the Roman force would have been able to make the last-minute preparations and adjustments that set the Roman army high above many of the other armies of the ancient world.

The XIIII Gemina, as the only full legion on the field, would have represented the core of the army. Once it had been allocated its forming-up point, it would have adopted the familiar double linear battle formation facing the enemy, with each cohort making for its own predetermined position in the line-up. The senior centurion of each cohort would then pass orders down directly from the Command group to the lower-ranking centurions responsible for the individual centuries that made up the unit. Soon the instructions would filter down until every contubernium was aware of its role in the coming fight.

As a full legion, XIIII Gemina would take precedence over the vexillation from Legion XX in the battle line, with the smaller group taking up a position behind the bigger unit. Its role would be to push the final charge forward from the rear, and in conjunction with the rear lines of the XIIII Gemina it would sweep away anything in its path as it picked up the irresistible momentum of the rolling charge. Next in the formation would come the auxiliary cavalry and infantry units, with the foot soldiers taking position on each flank while the cavalry formed up behind either side of the main body, waiting to stream out from behind the formation and carry out the typical Roman cavalry tactic of sweeping along the wings and then tearing into each flank of the enemy force with devastating effect.

Even though the Roman army appears to us today to be an incredibly complex organisation, with many of its elements subject to what we would consider to be very modern managerial and logistical concepts, its fighting strength was still made up of men who paid great deference to the many gods and goddesses who were part of the everyday life of a Roman citizen. As previously mentioned, they would have addressed their own individual spiritual needs by making offerings and praying to whichever deity, personal or role-specific, they had chosen to protect them. The more obvious gods, such as Mars or Jupiter, would be chosen for their ability to govern the course of the battle and strengthen the hand of the army. Then perhaps Victoria would have been invoked to make sure the Romans won the day. Finally the individual might have sought protection from deities such as Fortuna and Nemesis to ensure that fate and luck was on their side and that they would emerge from the battle unscathed.

With their personal ministrations taken care of, the army would then have turned to Paulinus. To him would fall the role of making a sacrifice to the gods prior to the battle and receiving the auspices that would indicate not only to him, but the whole army assembled before him, that the gods favoured them in the coming battle. In the presence of the entire army Paulinus would have invoked the gods and offered them incense and wine. Then, as the men watched eagerly, he would have sacrificed a beast such as an ox and then stood to one side, waiting expectantly as its liver was removed and the priest interpreted the message it contained. Further signs could be drawn from the flights of birds or other complex auspicious events in the near surroundings that only the suitably qualified priest could properly interpret. Then the decision of the gods would be given, and, no doubt to huge and relieved cheers, the priest would announce: 'The signs are good!' With due deference paid to matters spiritual, Paulinus would then have carried out the last duty expected of him by his men before battle was joined and he was caught up in the crucial task of directing his formations effectively. Now was the time to deliver his pre-battle speech.

Both Tacitus and Cassius Dio refer to the speeches made by Paulinus and Boudica on the eve of the battle. Tacitus offers two short but to-the-point speeches from each of the protagonists, whilst Cassius Dio, predictably, prefers to take a much more flamboyant approach to the matter of their delivery. In contrast to Tacitus's more economical account, Dio attributes three speeches to Paulinus, one for each division of the assembled force – no doubt represented by the legionaries, auxiliary infantry and cavalry. He does not, however, credit Boudica with a speech at this juncture, apparently relying on the queen's earlier speeches delivered on the eve of revolt to set the tone for the Britons.

It is most unlikely that either of these accounts give the actual words used in the speeches. The addresses are in fact well-placed literary devices which follow a set theme and have been used specifically to add a touch of drama and suspense for the reader. However, whilst the words within the two accounts can be safely regarded as the inventions of the writers, the importance of such speeches, to the Roman army at least, would have been crucial to both the performance and morale of the troops prior to going into battle. The appearance of the commander before the assembled troops would provide the men with the reassurance that their general was made of the same stuff as they were. He was there by their side, ready to fight and, if necessary, die alongside them. The address would also allow the commander the opportunity to fire his men up by decrying the abilities of the enemy against their own fighting skill and to appeal directly to their sense of honour, elements of which are clearly represented in the writings of Tacitus and Cassius Dio.

As for Boudica and her rebel army, both writers make reference to the problems caused by the baggage train that had apparently formed up behind the rebel force. This may indicate that the Britons did not rush pell-mell into the fight, suggesting instead that a degree of preparation took place in the rebel camp prior to the engagement. This pause would have allowed at least enough time to form the baggage train into an improvised viewing area where the non-combatant Britons could sit and watch their massive force crush the last vestiges of Roman dominance in Britain. Perhaps it was also the venue for one final speech by Boudica before she committed the force to its last fateful charge at the Roman lines.

THE KILLING GROUND

With both armies finally facing each other across open terrain, the time had now come for one of the commanders, Boudica or Paulinus, to make an initial move and commit to the battle.

From her position roughly a mile east of High Cross, Boudica would have seen her opponent's army on the crest of the rise, formed up in a great line 1,000 yards long, stretching from south of the Roman road junction to just a short distance north of it. On the northern extremity lay a newly constructed shallow ditch and rampart, running west to east and bristling along its top with *tribuli*, spiked barriers constructed from three sharpened wooden stakes lashed together and laid out with many others to form an almost impenetrable barrier for both infantry and cavalry. To the south was woodland, bolstered by the careful placement of more *tribuli*, covering Paulinus's other flank. The only option was to hit the waiting Roman line head-on, which to all intents and purposes was not going to be difficult, given that they seemed so few in number. It would appear almost guaranteed that the mighty force of assembled Britons would simply charge en masse up the gently sloping hill and sweep the troops aside. After that, Roman power in Britain would be finished.

Waiting silently at the top of the rise was Paulinus and his men. He would be willing the Britons to open hostilities with a mass charge, once they had seen his battle line and assumed that they were about to deal with a force not much bigger than the previous formation they had destroyed near Colchester. Once the Britons had committed to their charge and he had deployed his first row, then and only then would he commit the rest of the force, which was formed up just below the horizon that the Britons now saw before them. For now, though, they would wait, formed up out of sight towards Smockington Hollow, the natural feature revealed now as a plausible candidate for the defile mentioned in the account of Tacitus.

As a great roar rose from the assembled mass of Britons and their huge force began to roll towards the Roman lines, Paulinus made ready and watched, poised as the massive mob surged towards him, battle cries shattering the air and the thunder of hooves and chariot wheels blending with the deafening racket of swords and spears being rhythmically hammered on shields. Wild-looking Britons, some clad only in the swirling blue designs that adorned their bodies, rushed on flourishing their weapons and calling on their gods to bring victory over the Romans as they closed with the front rows of the waiting legionaries.

Silently the legionaries held their lines and steeled themselves, the men of the front rows watching as the chaotic mass surged towards them and the rear ranks listening to the approaching cacophony of sound – a continuous din heralding the arrival of a force that far outnumbered their own, probably in excess of ten to one. Here is where the iron discipline of the Roman troops paid dividends as the soldiers stood fast, despite feeling their bladders weaken and their stomachs knot with fear. As they gripped their weapons a little tighter to suppress the shaking of their hands they quietly placed their faith in the watching gods and the strategy of their commander. They took heart from the fact that, few though they might be, they were the best there was. If any army could win this day, it would be theirs. Besides, there was nowhere to run. If victory was denied them, they would at least die with honour.

In yet another brief but adequate account, Tacitus tells us what happened next. For all its brevity, this account is enough to be able to see how Paulinus could have achieved his stunning victory over such overwhelming numbers:

> At first the legionaries held their ground. Keeping to the defile as a natural defence, they launched their javelins accurately at the approaching enemy. Then, in wedge formation, they burst forward. So did the auxiliary infantry. The cavalry too, with their lances extended, demolished all resistance.
>
> (Tacitus, *Annals* XIV.36)

Tens of thousands of Britons would have been charging the Roman lines that day, and their numbers were not only made up of the nobility and warrior classes. Also in their huge army would have been the ordinary peasant, farmer or even skilled craftsman, all of them pushing themselves hard up the gentle slope towards the Roman formation as it stood motionless, the brightly coloured shield faces and shining armour stretching out in a great line, threatening, but at the same time infuriating the Britons who so keenly yearned to wipe it out once and for all. Swift, light chariots, pulled by stocky, hardy little ponies, would have thundered up to the line and deposited their warrior passengers into the fray while the fast-moving bands of cavalry bore down on the Romans in no particular order. Then, as the Britons closed with the Roman line, Paulinus would have given his carefully timed signal and the blaring notes of Roman horns would have risen over the din, signalling to the first row that now was the time to cast their weapons high.

A wave of heavy javelins, or *pila*, took to the air from behind the rows of shields. Timed to inflict the maximum devastation from their launch, the wickedly pointed shafts sliced swiftly through the air. With awesome effect, the great cloud of lethal missiles fell amongst the first lines of the charging rebels and the first screams of death and pain began to pierce the air as men and horses fell under the deadly hail. With its long slim tip of pointed iron pushed home by the momentum of its heavy wooden shaft, the Roman *pilum* was deadly. It could easily pierce the faces of the flat shields that the Britons carried and still follow through with enough kinetic energy to impale the man carrying it. If a *pilum* only pierced the shield it would usually become deeply lodged and force the bearer to discard the shield, which, with the long heavy shaft embedded in its face, had become more of a liability than an aid. If an enemy was unlucky enough not to be carrying a shield then there was little chance of survival if hit by this highly effective weapon.

With a long line of dead suddenly falling before them the Britons faltered, just long enough to allow the Romans to make their next move. Over the din of their own charge they would have heard the Roman legionaries roar out their defiance as each man simultaneously drew his *gladius* and slammed the blade of the wickedly sharp short sword into the side of his shield. Almost instantly, the supremely well-drilled soldiers would have fallen into position and formed up into dense wedges of around century strength. All along the front line they rapidly fell into formation before bursting forward, smashing into the rebels along the whole length of the Roman line and pushing outwards, battering their opponents with their shields and stabbing out with short, lethal thrusts. The wickedly pointed *gladius* would come into its own now as it punched out from the side of the *scutum* and jabbed into its victim, leaving gaping holes in soft abdominal flesh or bursting open the arteries in the neck, genitals, thigh or upper arm. Such simple but effective use of equipment allowed the wedges to maintain their forward momentum as they pushed down the slope and ripped through the massed ranks of Britons.

The shock of the wedge formations hitting the rebel force would have soon split the great mob into smaller groups as the wedges began to fragment the Britons and sow the seeds of panic amongst their numbers. The British warrior elite would have stood their ground and continued to press home their attack with typical ferocity, but they were few in number and the vast majority of the rebel force was ill equipped and undisciplined in the ways of war. Their ancient system would now be failing the rebels; with their chieftains starting to fall, the chiefs' clients would begin to waiver as they observed the Roman force chewing into their own, advancing with a ferocity and cold efficiency never encountered in those previous great victories that they had won over unprotected towns and an unwary marching column. To make matters even worse, while still desperately trying to recover from the impact of the devastating wedges of legionaries who were now ripping great swathes into their formation, the Britons would be shocked to see yet another great line of legionaries advancing over the crest of the rise and thundering towards them in a rolling charge down the slope, carving up the Britons who had made it through to the other side of the charging wedges. With the great mass now broken into smaller groups, the Britons were surprised and horrified by the appearance of the new formations bringing up the rear and taken aback by the ferocity of its impetus as it mowed everything down that stood in its way.

Any rebels out on the flanks would have also witnessed the arrival of the Batavian infantry on the field, rushing out in formation and clearing up the flanks of the rebel army, using their long swords to hack down any of the rebels as they tried to break off from the sides. The thunder of 1,000 auxiliary cavalry, 500 on each flank, rolling up the outside of the press and then turning inwards to set about slaughtering the packed crowds of rebels, was the final straw. Catastrophically, the British charge broke, and with many inexperienced fighters now in a desperate panic they turned and fled in droves.

The fugitives now began to run in all directions. The Britons were not just suffering casualties from Roman weapons, they were being crushed underfoot as many of them fell and were trampled to death or injured in the panic of the chaotic retreat. Many ran back towards their own baggage train where, a short while earlier, the now terrified and screaming non-combatants had howled and cheered as their army bore down on the Roman lines.

Stark panic gripped the Britons as the fleeing fighters, desperate to escape the rolling wall of armour, rushed towards the imagined safety of their own wagons and thereby unwittingly pulled the pursuing Roman force right into their midst. With nowhere to go, the trapped Britons were cut down without mercy as the Roman troops obeyed their instructions and swept through any and all who stood in their way. The result was absolute carnage. With each yard further down the slope, the bodies of the Britons lay in greater and greater numbers until they lay in great tangled heaps around the baggage train, slaughtered with their animals as the Roman juggernaut passed through. With the day now lost, the surviving Britons scattered.

RETRIBUTION

Paulinus had secured a stunning victory. Not only had he vanquished a force many times bigger than his own, he had also broken the back of a huge revolt that had almost toppled Roman rule and ended their occupation of Britain. The great mob that had fallen in behind Boudica was now in pieces and the queen herself was finished.

The classical accounts differ slightly as to what eventually became of Boudica after the battle, but it is certain that the Romans never got their trophy, alive or dead. Tacitus suggests that Boudica took poison after the battle, and Dio claims that she fell ill and died and was then given a lavish burial by her comrades. Perhaps the accounts are both correct, and the illness referred to by Cassius Dio was the result of self-administered poison that failed to act quickly; we will almost certainly never know for sure. However, the overall assertion that the defeated queen took her own life would make perfect sense if we consider her likely fate had she been taken alive by the Romans.

Far from being shown mercy and enjoying the same comfortable fate as Caratacus, her illustrious rebel predecessor, Boudica would have been made into a horrific example. As the instigator and ring leader of a revolt that, had it been successful, would have far surpassed the humiliation and loss that was caused by the Varus disaster, she would have suffered a very cruel and public ordeal. After a series of excruciatingly tortuous executions of her captured allies and, in her own case, being paraded in shackles through Britain and across Gaul, the rebel queen would have finally arrived in Rome. There she would have been tortured and humiliated to amuse the Roman mob and the imperial family before finally falling victim to her ultimate fate. Perhaps, like Vercingetorix before her, she would have remained a prisoner for years, held in humiliating squalor and broken of all pride before finally being publicly strangled in front of the good citizens of Rome. No doubt, after an unceremonious cremation, her ashes would have been dumped and word of the awful fate of an enemy of the state would have been sent around the empire, a warning to all would-be freedom fighters that any notion of rebellion was not worth the pain.

With the prospect of such a terrible end, the only option still open to Boudica would be to perform one last act which demonstrated that she was still in control of her own destiny: she would deny the Romans their triumph and kill herself. The beaten queen would have known that any attempt to escape and make a life elsewhere would not bring her peace; if the Romans knew she still lived they would not rest until they had hunted her down. Even Rome's greatest nemesis, Hannibal, was hounded to suicide as an old man, when the relentless pursuit finally came to an end and Roman troops discovered his final hiding place in Bithynia. As with him, a death by her own hand would be the only choice she could make.

Meanwhile, Paulinus still had much to do to restore order to the still simmering province of Britannia. With the fury of a man possessed, he began to squash any further likelihood of a new uprising.

In the immediate aftermath of the battle, according to Tacitus, around 80,000 rebels died on the field at a cost of some 400 Roman troops dead and a comparable number wounded. With the rebel body count standing at such a large number it at first seems unlikely that the Roman forces could possibly have emerged from the battle with so few losses. However, the only way that such a small force could have achieved such a resounding victory against such superior numbers was by shock tactics, hitting so hard and fast that their enemy was left reeling from the initial impact and given no time to recover. Once the head-on charge of the Britons had been broken it would then just be a matter of maintaining a swift advance and sweeping up the fleeing enemy, a tactic that would claim far fewer casualties on the Roman side than a toe-to-toe clash. Therefore, even if 400 dead is unlikely, the actual figure may not have been too much more than that.

Adding strength to this idea is the account given by Tacitus concerning the replenishment of the Roman garrisons in Britain after the revolt. Tacitus says that 2,000 regular troops were sent to replenish the losses of the IX Hispana along with eight auxiliary infantry cohorts and 1,000 cavalry. Clearly, had the XIIII Gemina and XX Legion been badly mauled in the engagement, extra troops would then have needed to be sent alongside the replacements for the IX Hispana. With the threat of the great mob and the rallying figurehead of Boudica now removed, Paulinus as yet felt no inclination to rest on his laurels, so to speak.

Many rebels had fled the field and still represented a very real danger, given that they could attempt to reignite the embers of the revolt. They would need to be swiftly hunted down and disposed of if proper order was to be reimposed and the Britons were to abandon any further ideas of rebellion. Besides, there was also the matter of punishment, something which would consume Paulinus so deeply that it would ultimately lead to his removal as governor.

Lists of names would have been drawn up from intelligence gathered by the Roman administration. This might have come from enterprising informants who recognised the futility of further disobedience and sought to make a few coins from their information, or from key players captured after the last battle and tortured to reveal the details that Paulinus sought. Again, it is Tacitus's *Annals* which provides the best description of what happened after the great battle was over. It is this account which speaks of Paulinus's newly reinforced army, operating from perhaps a central location and descending on the surrounding tribes to 'ravage them with fire and sword'.

It is clear that reprisals went on well into the winter of AD 61/62, as Tacitus confirms that the British tribes suffered famine as a result of neglecting to sow the annual crops, indicating that fighting had carried on well after the harvest time of late summer into early autumn. Even so, their hunger does not appear to have diminished their desire to defy Paulinus, and certain of the tribes continued to resist the campaign of terror that Paulinus was waging against them. It was this uncompromising and severe response after the battle that brought Paulinus into conflict with the replacement for Decianus, the previous imperial agent, and ultimately spelled the end of his time in Britain.

Gaius Julius Alpinus Classicianus, it would appear, was a man who had little time for Paulinus. The clear suggestion in Tacitus's account is that there was a good deal of personal enmity between him and Paulinus, and as soon as he took up the new appointment in Britain Classicianus eagerly embarked upon a point-scoring exercise against Paulinus which Tacitus suggests could have been very damaging to imperial interests in Britain. This included openly criticising the harshness of the follow-up action and undermining Paulinus, not only before British tribal representatives, but also in despatches to Rome which contained the clear suggestion that, while Paulinus still ran amok in Britain, there would be no end to the conflict.

Eventually Nero sent a court representative, the freedman Polyclitus, to Britain. His task was both to assess the situation in the province and to attempt to broker some sort of peace between the military governor and the new agent. It would seem, however, that Polyclitus's mission was a failure. The British tribes, unfamiliar with the strange goings on of the imperial Roman court and Roman society as a whole, could not reconcile themselves to the fact that a former slave not only held sway over such a powerful warrior as Paulinus but also possessed the immense personal wealth and power that he did. Seeing him as an alien figure, the Britons refused to take Polyclitus seriously, and the man was forced into sending despatches back to Rome which were heavily watered down and not representative of the actual picture in Britain at the time. As for Paulinus, he remained in post for a short while longer, probably until the early half of AD 62, when he was replaced by Publius Petronius Turpilianus, who had just completed a term in office as one of two annually appointed Imperial Consuls for the year AD 61. It was his arrival that finally heralded the end of the hostilities, thereby bringing the curtain down on one of the most remarkable chapters in British history.

Whilst it is the writings of Tacitus which have provided most of the detailed information concerning the revolt, perhaps it is fitting to end the story with the words of the other classical source, Cassius Dio. With a casually dismissive comment, Dio concludes his commentary: 'So much for the affair in Britain.'

8

AFTER THE FIRES

WINNERS AND LOSERS

It would seem that, after the final battle was fought, the army that had so recently won such an incredible victory was given very little chance to pause and consider just what they had managed to achieve. Paulinus, having then been in no mood to allow the surviving British rebels any respite, thrust his men straight into a bloody campaign of retribution that would, he resolved, finally rid the occupied territories of any further ideas of revolt. When it was eventually over, all of the key Roman players then drifted on to other posts and appointments and eventually faded from prominence.

Gaius Suetonius Paulinus, military governor of Britannia and one of the finest generals of his age, was, after his replacement by Turpilianus, recalled to Rome by Nero. His next notable mention comes in AD 66 when he was then appointed to one of the two annual posts of Consul, alongside Caius Luccius Telesinus. A few years later, in a rather ignominious fall from grace, Paulinus became involved in the dramatic power struggles of AD 69. Unfortunately, Paulinus backed the cause of Marcus Salvius Otho against his rival Aulus Vitellius. Having been given command of Otho's forces, he initially secured a victory against the Vitellian forces at Cremona. Vitellius however later defeated Otho, and it is here that the story of Paulinus is finally lost to us. Having received an official pardon for his involvement with Otho, Paulinus then quietly slipped into the shadows of history. How curious it seems that of the two main rivals involved in the Boudican revolt it is the heavily outnumbered Roman general, who managed to turn an almost certain defeat into a resounding victory, who has become the figure less remembered in popular history.

And what of Cerialis? Despite having stumbled into an ambush that cost him the greater part of half a legion, Quintus Petillius Cerialis does not appear to have ever been held personally responsible for such a serious loss. Indeed, his subsequent military career turned out to be very much a distinguished one. By the fateful year of AD 69, Cerialis was active in assisting Vespasian to capture Rome. The following year, in a strange twist of fate involving two veteran units of the Boudican revolt, he found himself commanding the XIIII Gemina in Germany against the Batavians who had risen up in revolt under the leadership of Julius Civilis. After the successful suppression of the Batavian revolt, Cerialis returned to Britain and once more resumed command of his old legion, the IX Hispana. Quite what the soldiers thought of being led once more by a legate who had brought such a terrible defeat on them will never be known. He nonetheless used them to decisive effect, along with Legio II Adiutrix, to put an end to the revolt of the Brigantean confederation led by Venutius. The pinnacle of Cerialis's achievements in Britain, and his last significant mention in the history books, was his eventual appointment as governor, a post he held from AD 71 until around AD 74, after which he was finally recalled to Rome.

Although nothing is yet certain concerning the identity of the auxiliary units that took part in the final battle, we can be sure about the involvement of the two legions, the XIIII Gemina and the XX Legion. In mentioning the involvement of the entire XIIII Gemina during the Boudican revolt, Tacitus provides one of only a handful of written and inscriptional references that even attest to the presence of the legion in Britain. In general the details of their service in the province are obscure, and there is little that can be said for certain concerning their movements. It is known, however, that in recognition of their service during the Boudican revolt the legion was awarded the additional titles of 'Martia' and 'Victrix', which then provided them with their full, more familiar title of the 14th twin legion that is martial and victorious – or, in its abbreviated form, LEG XIIII GMV.

In AD 64 the legion was sent back to the Rhineland by the Emperor Nero to assist in defending Roman territorial interests against hostile tribes active along the Rhine frontier. It was here in AD 69 that Cerialis led them against the revolt of Civilis and the Batavians. The legion is known to have subsequently been stationed at its former base in Mogontiacum, then Vindobona and finally Carnuntum, before its name is temporarily lost to history.

If a certain degree of obscurity exists concerning the activities of the XIIII GMV in Britain then the same certainly cannot be said about the XX Legion. As one of the best-known and well-evidenced legions ever to have served in Britain, the story of this particular legion is much easier to trace. As well as historical texts, a wealth of inscriptional information is available which charts the movements of the legion as it conducted operations along almost the entire length of Roman-occupied Britain. After taking part in the decisive battle against Boudica the legion was awarded honorary titles similar to those bestowed upon the XIIII GMV, these being 'Valeria' and 'Victrix', or valiant and victorious. In the years following the revolt the legion was garrisoned in the biggest legionary fortress in Britain, Deva Victrix, now known as Chester. It saw action against the Brigantean rebels under Venutius and carried out construction work and garrison postings along both the Antonine Wall and Hadrian's Wall. Along the way they left behind a wealth of archaeology, which has since assisted modern scholars and historians to piece together not only the movements of the legion but also the lives of some of the thousands of men who saw service in its illustrious ranks.

As for the Britons, it is ironic that, for all that the Romans mostly regarded them as uncultured barbarians who occupied a mysterious and wild land on the edge of the known world, they were eventually drawn into the Roman ideal of civilisation. After years of resistance they finally came to embrace the notion of becoming Romanised, and subsequently evolved into a shining example of how well Roman provincialism worked. Commercial interests thrived both at home and abroad as the new British entrepreneurs shared the marketplace of the empire with traders from all over the known world. The Roman push for urbanisation in the new province saw the rise of great Romano-British towns and cities, many of which still endure today. The Britons also benefited heavily from the importation of new trades. With the advent of the Pax Romana in Britain came new crafts and skills, many of which were first introduced by the brutally efficient Roman troops. The ongoing development of these skills ensured that home-grown tradesmen such as stonemasons, artists and mosaicists produced work on a level of excellence almost comparable to their Mediterranean counterparts. Industry and agriculture were also brought right up to date with the appliance of more efficient Roman technology. All the while, those who had been far-sighted enough to embrace the coming of Rome now reaped their rewards with new and golden opportunities. Effectively they became the nouveau riche of Roman Europe. As great new towns and cities sprung up out of the landscape, the traditional old roundhouses that were a symbol of the past gave way to smart new country villas. The old life was soon forgotten and swapped for a smart new toga and underfloor heating as the once feudal chieftains took a Latinised name and concentrated on the business of making money. Eventually these once insular people would become the fat cat capitalists of a new, booming Britain.

As perhaps the supreme irony, it was the flashpoint of the Boudican revolt that finally brought the situation in Britain to a head. Inadvertently, the rebellion allowed the Romans to clear the decks of any serious opposition to their rule. Of course, there were many more years of conquest still to be accomplished, as the Romans steadily spread their control north, but nothing on the threat scale of the great revolt would ever emerge to resist their advance again. Eventually the conquest would be complete and Rome would then control a vast chunk of Britain for another 350 years. Finally they chose to abandon the province to its fate only when its own existence was threatened by the advance of barbarian tribes.

It has been said that there was little benefit to be had for the ordinary people of Britain from the new Roman regime, as they knuckled under to the laws and taxes of the new order. Theirs was a life of toiling for long hours in workshops and fields to scrape a living for themselves and their families. There would probably never be any chance of sharing in the new-found prosperity that was now providing a fortunate few with a very good standard of living. Poverty, disease, and hunger were always constant spectres in the lives of the lower classes, and their avoidance depended chiefly on being able to produce certain commodities that they could trade for their continued livelihoods.

However, in the final analysis, was the situation ever any different for the ordinary folk under their old masters? Taxation, as Caesar points out, was a burden to them even before the arrival of the Romans, and life would always be hard for those born outside the privileged classes. They were always going to be nothing more than servants, vassals to a master who could be cruel or kind. That was never a purely Roman innovation. Perhaps it would be more positive to think that, for all of the changes that Roman rule brought with it, some of those benefits did eventually percolate down to the ordinary people after all – even if it were only, say, a new farming method to improve crop yields. That at least would have had a positive effect on the lives of ordinary Britons who relied on such yields to see them through another year.

A WORTHY OPPONENT

Far from being a wanton rampage of destruction and revenge, or even a spontaneous act of mindless violence, hurriedly orchestrated by a grieving widow and mother who had been so terribly wronged, the Boudican revolt was a far more calculating affair. It was more like a deliberate and premeditated act of war, in fact, with clearly defined and well-planned objectives.

Acting as the catalyst which triggered the revolt, the wrongs done to the Iceni and their royals by the Roman administration saw Boudica placed at the head of a rebellion that in reality had been simmering for some time. Not only did the greed of Decianus push the Iceni too far, it unwittingly also created a perfect figurehead to encourage and inspire the would-be rebels. With Boudica came a focus for all of the peoples of Britain who had fallen under the heel of the Roman boot. Inspired by the example of her righteous indignation, they resolved to take back control of their own destiny and live free once more, just as they had before the legions arrived on their shores.

Though it is the name of Boudica which echoes down through the ages, the various successful phases of the revolt must also be attributed to an assembly of other, as yet unidentified, British chieftains – tribal leaders who, finding their lives driven by a common goal, elected to put aside the feuds of the past and instead work together. Once they had been enemies, but now they were encouraged to form an uneasy alliance to rid themselves of their hated new masters. During the course of many secretive meetings over many months, they forged a complex plan which, by the final dramatic act, very nearly achieved its objective.

With so many different factions thrashing out agreement on the various points, it would be unthinkable to suggest that it was accomplished without the collaboration of the order of Druids. For so long they had acted as both mediators and arbiters between the various factions that represented the population of Britain.

Their input would be crucial in brokering any agreement with kings and chieftains who would normally not think twice about going to war with their neighbour if the need arose. With the Druids able to move freely between the various factions, they would have been welcome everywhere they went and would no doubt have worked tirelessly to achieve an agreement between the tribes. They were, after all, in very real danger of being wiped out by the Romans and the success of the planned revolt was going to be very much a matter of survival for them.

Knowing that there was no going back once they had set out upon the path to war, the rebels swiftly achieved the first of their objectives. The fall of Camulodunum not only secured a devastating opening victory which yielded valuable tactical benefits, it also gave the oppressed Britons their first heady taste of the sweet revenge that fuelled the fire in the ordinary Britons – folk who had suffered for years under the burden of Roman taxation, arrogance and callous brutality.

As the revolt gained pace, more evidence of forward planning, as opposed to spontaneous action, presents itself with the destruction of the IX Hispana battle group. This crucial victory could only have been secured by Boudica and the rebel leaders actively monitoring the developing situation carefully and then deciding to play to the enemy's weakness. Only by successfully identifying the fact that the mighty Roman army was never as vulnerable as when it was on the march would the rebels know what strategy to use. While the growing rebel force was still fairly inexperienced, a hard-hitting ambush would be the only way to take on and defeat such a potent fighting force as nearly half a legion of campaign-hardened soldiers. Boudica and her lieutenants would have realised that, once the approaching formation had been removed from the picture, a whole host of advantages would then present themselves.

Again, evidence for Boudica and her lieutenants thinking tactically becomes apparent with the destruction of London. Not only was this seemingly unimportant commercial centre utterly destroyed, any efforts that could have been launched from the south to send aid to Paulinus would have been seriously hampered by the destruction wrought on the helpless town. Apart from the opportunity to kill, burn and loot, it would hardly seem worth the lengthy diversion needed to attack London first rather than make straight for the former Catuvellaunian capital of St Albans, unless the attack promised to achieve more than simple destruction. With the town in flames, its warehouses destroyed and supplies looted to feed the rebel advance, the Boudican host then took out the only crossing of the Thames for many miles in either direction before moving on to the last of their big successes: the attack on Verulamium.

Could it really be that these important advantages were just the chance by-product of a disorganised rampage? Or is it now becoming clear that, far from acting like the revenge-driven barbarians that they are so often painted as, the Boudican rebels conducted their campaign in a much more adroit manner than was first thought? The reality seems to be that the rebellious tribespeople had made every effort to control the pace of the revolt to their advantage. Their devastating opening attacks served both to cut off any chance of assistance for Paulinus and reduce the likelihood of an attack from the rear. This served not only to close down the options for the Roman force, which the Britons knew they would eventually have to meet, but also to buy them valuable time to form new alliances and swell their numbers to the extent that nothing would be able to stand in their way once they decided to move north.

If Boudica had managed to secure just one more alliance, perhaps with the Coritani as suggested, it is just possible that the ultimate outcome would have been very different to the one with which we are now so familiar. In the end it seems that the only way for the rebels to have had the chance to succeed was for all of them to fully embrace the unfamiliar concept of tribal unity, something that was very much at odds with their heritage and culture. Ultimately this fact would have spelt Boudica's undoing, as the various tribes within the massive rebel force eventually reverted to type and fragmented into the assembly of disparate peoples that they were. As it was, her failure ensured that the influence of Roman culture would become the foundation of the British nation of today, and, ironically, that the pacified British tribes would eventually become a united and centrally governed people.

If she had ever managed to achieve the ultimate goal of vanquishing the forces of Rome then there is no doubt that the name of Boudica would still be just as well known today, purely because she would have managed to free herself and her people from the clutches of Rome – something that very few people were ever able to achieve. It is very likely that had she beaten the Romans, she would have initially taken a position as the overall leader of a mighty federation of recently liberated tribes who, now united in the euphoria of victory, would then have paused and taken stock of their situation. Eventually the victorious rebels would cast their eye once more over the tribes that had not supported them. A fresh war may well have then loomed as the old enemies of tribes such as the Dobunni, Cantiaci, Regni, and Atrebates found even more strength than they had wielded previously and set out to visit retribution on those who had collaborated with Rome. In addition, Cartimandua of the Brigantes may well have come to be regarded as the next great threat; a collaborator and betrayer of her own kind, she also happened to control the only other large tribal confederation in Britain. War with the Brigantes may have followed, and eventually the unity that had brought about victory over Rome would have begun to crumble as individual tribes, realising now that they could resume their old lives, began to serve their own interests once more and quickly forgot any further notions of unity.

Had this been the case, Boudica would certainly have been remembered as a true queen, the first to be recorded in British history and an inspirational leader who united the tribes, took on Rome, and won their freedom. Ultimately, however, she would probably also be remembered for a brief but turbulent reign as an emerging nation took its first faltering steps and then stumbled and fell, taking the great queen with it. As the factionalism of the old culture kicked in once more, Boudica would have been unable to grip the reins of power any longer and the idea of a united Britain would have faded away. Such a nation would probably then only be destined to re-emerge under the influence of another group of invaders from over the seas who would, like the Romans before, have struggled to instil their own culture and values on a collection of people who did not want to change – a people who now knew, from the lessons of history, that they had the power to resist if the need ever again arose.

With the Romans leaving prematurely, a different Britain to that of today would have emerged from history, perhaps as a society that mirrored that of its cousins in Ireland. The alternative Britain would still have had a certain amount of its history committed to record by the Romans, but the rest would have come down to us through the centuries as magical folk tales. Just as in Ireland, the tradition of oral transmission by the great Celtic storytellers would have taken precedence over the written methods of record keeping so favoured by its continental neighbours, and the ancient law of the Druids would have finally won out. Again, just like Ireland, the influences over the centuries from invaders such as the Vikings and Normans would have still found their way into the national identity, but the strongest of all influences would have been Celtic. With the foundation British culture firmly based on Celtic society, the influence of Rome would have been far weaker, and that, in turn, would have probably seen Britain creating a very different place for itself in the world than the one it currently enjoys today. The alternative Britain would have perhaps been a more spiritual society, and it would almost certainly have trailed behind developmentally as the rest of Roman Europe left it to its own devices while its culture evolved from a set of ideals based on the classical model that still pervades our lives today.

As it was, Boudica lost her fight and Britain remained a province of Rome, embracing her language and culture for nearly 400 years. However, when the shadow of Rome had eventually faded away and Britain was finally left to its fate, the history books had by then already been written. They would come to guarantee Boudica the place in the annals of world history that she so richly deserves.

Why then does Boudica command such interest? Essentially, she was an unimportant tribal queen from a backwater province whom history could so easily have passed by. And yet there is an endless list of books, plays, poetry, and film and TV projects available to us that, in some way or other, strive to shed light on the life of a woman about whom history can tell us almost nothing. It is only Tacitus and Cassius Dio who mention her in detail, and other than the information contained in their accounts we know nothing of her. We certainly cannot rely entirely on the accuracy of the fiercely intimidating Amazon as described by Cassius Dio. However, that very image is the one with which the queen is now firmly associated, even though Dio probably created it as a composite of what he knew of British noble women, combined with descriptive elements that he was sure would excite the imagination of his readers. Modern works which offer details such as her age, physical description or personality traits can only do so in the knowledge that the picture they are painting of the queen is a purely speculative one. Sometimes the work is based on sound research and reasoning and other times not, but always her true nature eludes the would-be biographer.

In searching for the key points that make Boudica's story so captivating, it becomes evident that it shares common ground with two of her contemporaries. The first was Caratacus, a noble prince and warrior and a great British rebel, who held out against Rome for years as an underdog fighting to regain the freedom and independence that his people had so recently lost. Secondly, Cartimandua was another powerful British queen who commanded a large confederation of tribes. Her story is spiced up by the guaranteed crowd-pleasers of sex, intrigue, and betrayal. However, neither of these figures enjoys anything like the same level of popularity that Boudica continues to command. Her story is not only a potent mix of the aforementioned elements, it is also representative of a mother's basic instinct to protect her children and home, whatever the odds against her might be.

That Boudica is many things to many different people is obvious. It is therefore unlikely that any commentator could venture to offer a critique of the queen which was universally accepted by all of those many people, academic, and layman alike, who continue to be so enthralled by both the woman and her story. Given the many facets to her story, it is doubtful that she will ever lose her appeal, just as it is doubtful that we will ever have all of the answers to all of the questions we have ever asked about her. With so much of her story still shrouded in mystery, perhaps it is the deeply enigmatic nature of the life and times of Britain's first great queen that will ultimately command our interest for many years to come, as we continue to explore the legend that is Boudica, Queen of the Iceni.

APPENDIX 1

Note: The figures and equipment shown in the illustrations are specifically intended to reflect the various patterns likely to be in use in Britain at the time of the Boudican revolt. They should therefore not be viewed as more general figure types.

FIGURE A. CENTURION

Generally speaking, the overall title of centurion has no modern military rank equivalent. The centurionate was a multi-layered ranking system that encompassed a great many roles at various levels of seniority. It is only when the individual appointments within the structure are examined that approximate modern equivalents can be attributed to the ancient role.

The figure illustrated represents a centurion in charge of a century of Cohors III Legio XIIII GEM. This particular soldier is from a first-line cohort, indicating a reasonably senior status within the body of the legion, and his equipment is typical of what one would usually accept to be a generic representation of a centurion.

Perhaps the most prominent feature of his kit is the crest, or *crista transversa*, which runs crossways over the helmet. The helmet itself is a Gallic type which has been tinned and further embellished with decorative motifs to the cheek guards.

The ring mail shirt, or *lorica hamata*, worn here is made of three-millimetre internal diameter iron rings, each of which has been individually riveted together. Other production methods for these shirts involved fusion welding of the rings or die-punching solid rings from iron sheet. This particular shirt is a very expensive piece that only a centurion was likely to be able to afford, given that he was typically paid around fifteen times more salary than a legionary. To increase the protective properties of the mail a leather garment, or *subarmalis*, is worn under the shirt. This is evidenced by the pendulous leather straps known as *pteruges*, which can be seen covering the upper arms and thigh area. If the *subarmalis* is not worn, the protective qualities of the mail have been proven in modern tests to be much reduced.

Worn over the top of the shirt is a leather harness that holds what are in effect the campaign medals won by the soldier during his service. These decorations, or *phalerae*, have been found in various forms, but the types illustrated are the most common and are generally fabricated from metals such as bronze or brass which are then silvered. In this case they are accompanied by a pair of silver torques worn suspended around the neck. These torques are also service awards and, along with the *phalerae*, are clearly represented on many of the surviving tombstones of centurions. *phalerae* are generally shown worn in sets of five, seven, nine, and so on.

Two other badges of office shown are the *vitis*, or vine staff and shin greaves, or *ocreae*. The *vitis* is known from classical records to have been used by the centurion to administer both spontaneous and formal punishment beatings. As mentioned earlier, excessive use of the *vitis* was probably the overriding factor in prompting the murder of the centurion known as *cedo alteram*, and may lead one to conclude that overuse of the staff was not as frequent as has been suggested. The greaves worn are of a simple pattern, and are again finished with a plating of tin. Greaves can be extremely ornate in their design and the more elaborate varieties were obviously an expensive piece of equipment. This fact, combined with their minimal protective qualities, suggests that they were worn more as another badge of office rather than for any practical purpose.

The centurion shown is carrying a Mainz pattern *gladius*, or short sword, which is held in a scabbard, or *vagina*, decorated with chased and silvered plates. This older pattern sword is likely to have been the centurion's primary weapon from the time he was a young legionary, one which he has maintained throughout his service and decorated as he could afford it. Unlike the legionary, the centurion wears his sword on his left side. Centurions are also generally seen wearing open toed boots, or *calceii*, although in this case he has retained the use of the standard military boots, or *caligae*.

FIGURE B. LEGIONARY

The legionary shown here is wearing *lorica segmentata*, a type of body armour constructed from iron plates that have been riveted to internal leather straps. This method of construction allows the armour a high degree of articulation and, if correctly sized to the individual, affords the wearer a reasonable degree of comfort. This particular pattern, Corbridge type B, uses a system of hooks and eyelets to secure the shoulder sections to the girdles. It is then done up using a strap and buckle to the front and rear to secure the upper sections, with lacings through bronze loops used to fasten the girdle sides together.

As a protection system the armour was extremely effective against both stabs and chopping blows, but it required a high degree of maintenance due to its many component parts. As time progressed and the armour type evolved, its design became much less elaborate, as evidenced by the later Newstead patterns. The Corbridge B shown here is a good example of the middle phases of the evolution of this type of armour, as it uses far fewer of the strap and buckle fastenings which are prone to failure. They are instead replaced by the aforementioned hooks and eyes, which have been proven more durable and easier to replace. The B type does retain the eight hinges on the shoulder plates, which were later phased out in favour of a more solid riveted construction. These hinges were time-consuming to manufacture and were a weak component that was difficult to replace or repair.

Although *lorica segmentata* is possibly the type of armour most commonly worn by the legionary, it should be emphasised that legionaries also wore other types such as ring mail and scale mail, or *lorica squamata*, during this period.

An iron Gallic type G helmet provides the legionary with his head protection. Although appearing elaborate, these helmets were very advanced in their protective qualities. The thick iron brow guard protected from downward strikes to the head while shaped cheek pieces and a broad neck guard served to protect the face and major blood vessels of the neck. Bronze flanges around the ear ports allowed the ear to be left partially exposed, which meant the soldier's ears were protected but still allowed him to hear what was going on. Although impressively ornate, the designs pushed out of the metal, such as the work on the cheek pieces and the eyebrow designs on the helmet bowl, actually contributed to the rigidity of the metal, thereby adding further strength to the fabric of the helmet.

The legionary shown carries a *gladius* of the Pompeii pattern, worn on his right side. This weapon is primarily a stabbing sword, which was typically deployed in precise, energy-efficient thrusts from behind the shield. The legionary was trained to become deadly efficient in its use during repeated drills and exercises, as he was with all of his personal equipment. He also carries a heavy iron dagger, or *pugio*, again primarily intended for stabbing; this is shown suspended from mounts on his military belt, or *cingulum militare*. This belt was often very ornately decorated with belt plates in numerous styles involving processes such as casting, plating, engraving, and enamelling. The front apron must only realistically be considered as decorative and is of a style common to the period in question, although by the time of the Emperor Trajan they had become much shorter and eventually disappeared altogether, perhaps suggesting a more symbolic use than a practical one.

The *pilum* or heavy javelin shown in the illustration was effective at ranges of around twenty to thirty metres. It consisted of a wooden shaft onto which an iron tip was mounted. When thrown, the weight of the weapon provided it with a powerful delivery onto its target where it was able to pierce armour such as ring mail and punch its way through shields. The square-section iron tip meant that the weapon was very difficult to remove from a shield and this would often force the bearer to discard it, leaving him vulnerable to any subsequent waves thrown and without protection in single combat. The two pins that secured the iron tip to the wooden shaft were easily removable, meaning that any damaged weapons collected after battle could quickly be repaired using pre-prepared iron tips to replace bent or broken ones.

The legionary *scutum*, or shield, is an extremely versatile piece of equipment which the legionary was able to use in a variety of deployments. Its hemicylindrical shape allowed it to be held very close into the body, offering maximum protection to front and sides, while its three-ply strip wood construction afforded it great strength. As well as being able to form shield walls and the famous overhead *testudo* formation, the shield also made an effective weapon as the legionary could punch out with the heavy iron boss or *umbo* and jab out with the bronze encased edges. The painted design on the front identifies the soldier as a member of LEG XIIII GEM.

To reflect the inclement conditions prevailing in Britain, and the likely Germanic origins of this particular soldier, the figure shown is wearing leggings referred to as *feminalia*. This name may be a reference to the femur and the fact that the leggings only cover the thigh area, although it has been suggested that the term indicates that the wearer is displaying feminine attributes and is unmanly, as the wearing of leggings was considered effeminate by the Romans. This suggestion does however seem somewhat flawed, given both the nature of the clothing styles of the diverse cultures that were eventually encompassed by the empire and the different climatic conditions under which the soldiers were expected to operate in the various theatres to which they were posted. It would therefore seem more sensible to table the suggestion that a practically minded soldier was more inclined to wear what afforded him the most comfort and practicality, rather than worry over what people thought. As well as a woollen tunic, the soldier is also wearing a hooded woollen cloak or *paenula*, which would no doubt have been essential wear in the often cold and wet conditions of Britain.

The legionary is also wearing the standard military boots, or *caligae*, which even in wet conditions are an effective piece of footwear. The open design has been proven to afford the wearer fewer problems than an enclosed boot as water drains quickly from the shoe and allows both the leather and the foot to dry out quicker, thereby preventing such conditions as trench foot. Extra warmth for the feet was also provided by the wearing of woollen socks, or *udones*, if required.

FIGURE C. AUXILIARY INFANTRYMAN

The term 'auxiliary' is used to refer to a wide range of soldiers used by the Roman army, drawn from all over the conquered territories of the empire. The description not only covers various types of infantry and cavalry but also such specialists as archers and slingers.

The figure shown represents a light infantryman from the territories of northern Gaul or the Rhineland. His clothing and equipment, although normally considered standard kit for this type of soldier, is therefore actually reflective of his cultural and ethnic origins. The retention and continued use of such equipment was probably a crucial factor in transplanting the fighting effectiveness of non-citizen or Peregrine troops into the ranks of the Roman army and negated the need to re-train newly levied men in new and unfamiliar weapons.

The soldier shown is wearing an auxiliary type B helmet made from bronze. Although much more basic in its pattern than many contemporary legionary helmets, its design still employs the basic protective features such as a broad neck guard, wide cheek pieces and an added brow protector. He is also wearing a basic pattern short-sleeved shirt of mail, which again would most probably be worn over a sub-garment to augment its protective qualities. Added personal protection is then drawn from the oval shield, or *clipeus*, that he is carrying. This shield is a flat oval of wood, trimmed on this occasion in brass and fitted with a bronze boss. Although perhaps less versatile than the legionary *scutum*, it is lighter and less cumbersome, complementing the soldiers' role of acting as fast-moving light infantry and skirmishers.

His weapons include a stabbing spear, or *hasta*, which is retained to stab at opponents rather than to be thrown as a missile. This gives the soldier the advantage of reach when engaging enemies with short hand-held blades, and also in countering mounted opponents. His primary weapon is an iron long sword, or *spatha*, which, in contrast to the *gladius*, is deployed in a slash-and-chop style. This method reflects the style of fighting common to the tribes of northern Europe and dictated many of the design characteristics of Roman protective equipment such as brow guards and mail shoulder doublings. He also carries an iron dagger which, along with his *spatha*, is suspended from a pair of decoratively plated belts.

A woollen tunic and full-length trousers, or *bracchae*, complete his soft clothing while his feet are protected by fully enclosed boots or *perones*.

FIGURE D. AUXILIARY CAVALRYMAN

As with the infantry, the auxiliary cavalry units of the Roman army differed widely in their roles and styles, depending on their country of origin. Many types were available including heavy, light, and even mounted archers.

The illustration shows a trooper from a Gallic cavalry unit, representing the type of equestrian warrior so admired by Julius Caesar during the Gallic Wars. As skilled and brave horsemen they eventually became part of the Roman war machine, forming extremely effective units capable of delivering deadly support to infantry operations.

The trooper shown is mounted on a short, stocky pony that may have been shipped over from Gaul once it had been broken and trained. In the absence of stirrups, the rider stayed on his mount by bracing himself on a specially designed saddle that had a protruding horn at each corner of the seat. Modern trials of reconstructed Roman saddles have demonstrated that these horns allowed the rider to wedge himself firmly into position, affording him maximum stability and control both at the gallop and in the deployment of his weapons.

His personal protection consists of an auxiliary cavalry type B helmet, an example of which was recovered from Witcham Gravel, Ely, Cambridgeshire. The helmet has an iron skull and cheek pieces and is further adorned with yellow bronze fittings with punched decorative patterns. His body armour is a ring mail shirt fitted with an extra layer of mail known as a Gallic cape. This extra protection was probably intended to reduce the injuries sustained from downward sword blows when the rider engaged in swordplay with opposing cavalry. Additional protection is provided by the *clipeus* carried by the rider.

His sword is the *spatha*, which is the same type as that carried by the auxiliary infantryman. This long-bladed weapon would have been ideal for mounted usage, as its length would have negated the necessity for the rider to lean too far out of his centre of balance in order to engage foot soldiers, thereby reducing the risk of being unhorsed. The spear was fitted with a slightly longer shaft than the *hasta* used by the infantry, and is most usually shown, on reliefs and the like, as being used in an overarm stabbing motion, which probably allowed the rider to exert greater force in the delivery of the strike.

His clothing consists of a long-sleeved woollen top, which extends to the hip area, and a pair of leggings made from wool or soft leather. These would have been a necessity for protecting the skin of the legs while mounted in the horns of the saddle for long periods of time.

FIGURE E. ICENIAN NOBLE

Either on the battlefield or on state occasions, the appearance of a warrior accoutred in this manner would instantly convey to all present that the wearer was a person of substance. By donning such clothing, jewellery and weaponry the wearer is making a deliberate show of wealth and power that few ordinary tribespeople would even dare to aspire to, let alone be capable of attaining.

His clothing is made from the finest textiles available, with extravagant use of expensive checked patterns probably imported from Gaul. His tunic has been dyed with woad and trimmed with fine tablet-woven appliqués around the hems, while his boots have been crafted from best-quality leather. As an affluent noble, his monetary wealth is conspicuously displayed the thick gold torque around his neck. This is an item he could probably easily afford to surrender several times over to the gods in the form of a votive offering, similar to those found at Snettisham in Norfolk.

The possession of items of armour and weaponry also indicates great wealth and status. The mail shirt would have been a highly prized and astronomically expensive piece of equipment, matched only by the finely crafted iron sword, sheathed in a fine bronze scabbard and suspended from a bronze sword chain. The leaf-shaped iron spearhead mounted on an ash shaft is another expensive item, beyond the reach of many ordinary Britons.

This noble also wears a very expensive helmet, probably imported from Gaul. By its style it would probably be classed as an antique by this time; it is a relic of the late Republican to early Augustan period and is of the Montefortino pattern. It is fashioned from bronze that has been silvered and then decorated with a horsehair crest. Completing the display is a large shield made from thin oak planks covered in leather. The spine and boss is of timber, hollow at the centre to accommodate a handgrip and sheathed in a strip of iron for added reinforcement. A hide edging has been applied on this particular example and the face has been decorated with motifs commonly found on coins of the Iceni tribe.

FIGURE F. BRITISH WAR CHARIOT

Far from being the large, lumbering vehicles suggested by some Hollywood productions and the Thorneycroft statue, the British war chariot is now known to have been a technologically advanced piece of equipment for its time, and an important component in the tribal armies of Britain. The lightweight chariot was capable of serving as a swift and stable platform which could deliver warriors into the heart of a fight before swiftly withdrawing and waiting on the edge of the conflict before returning and then retrieving warriors from the battlefield. In addition, according to Caesar, it could inject panic and chaos amongst Roman troops unused to facing such machines.

Although the use of the chariot is documented in classical records, very little is known for certain about its construction. However, a British war chariot was recently reconstructed for a British TV documentary, which must be the closest interpretation yet of of how such machines were constructed and functioned.

In 2001 a chariot burial was excavated at Wetwang in East Yorkshire. Evidence from the grave, along with other sources of information, allowed a team of specialists to assemble a very credible reconstruction of one of these vehicles. The end result was a chariot that was light, fast and manoeuvrable, while stable enough to allow the use of weapons such as javelins whilst on the move. The team believed that the inverted 'Y' shape within the double hoops along the sides of the chariot, as seen on many contemporary coins, was not a timber frame but in fact leather strapping from which the floor of the chariot was suspended. As the reconstruction demonstrated, this provided a smooth, stable platform for the driver and accompanying warrior. The team also put forward credible proposals on the arrangement of harness and tack and the construction and mounting of the spoked wheels. The addition of a pair of ponies, closely resembling the type of horse that the Britons would have used, further served to demonstrate what the chariot could achieve in the hands of a skilled crew.

Although the burial of the chariot at Wetwang occurred over 200 years before the Boudican revolt, it is hard to see how such a machine could really have been improved upon in the intervening years. The chariots faced by Paulinus's army may therefore have looked and operated very much like the one reconstructed from the evidence of the Wetwang burial. However, modern estimates indicate that such a machine may have taken a native artisan around a year to build. Combined with the fact that the Roman administration had imposed sweeping prohibitions on the possession of weapons by Britons, this may lead one to conclude that very few of these machines were actually present at the last battle.

FIGURE G. TRIBAL CHAMPION

Perhaps the archetypal image of the Celtic warrior is that represented by this illustration of the tribal champion. However, whilst it is tempting to imagine a Celtic army comprised of a vast horde of such warriors, the truth is rather less exotic.

As explained earlier, the bulk of any tribal army was comprised of simple tribespeople who had been assembled under the direction of their lord, who was in turn bound by clientage to a more powerful chieftain. This was repeated up through the hierarchy to the ruling family of the tribe. Large groups of ordinary people, poorly equipped and not properly trained in the ways of war, were thus in the position of being led by a small, elite band of warrior champions and ruling nobility.

The champion illustrated here embodies the code of conduct observed by such warriors. He stands alone and defiant on the battlefield and is calling for a champion of the opposing army to come forth and engage in single combat. The outcome of such a duel could then decide the dispute that has brought the two forces to the brink of armed conflict, and thus avoid the need for total war.

Having discarded his shield and armour and stripped to the waist, the champion is proclaiming both his skill as a fighter and his lack of concern for injury and death, since he believes that his mortal passing is not the end and that his soul will soon return to live in another incarnation. The strength of this belief makes him a determined and fearless opponent as he crosses the field armed only with his sword, in the knowledge that he has proven himself a worthy champion by defeating the challenge of his tribal peers and winning the right to call out an opposing champion on behalf of his tribe.

An important part of the champion's battlefield ritual again involves display. When calling out his opponent the champion will hurl insults at the enemy and brag of the many victories he has won in an attempt to intimidate his foe. These displays of arrogant bravado are combined with the physical presence he commands, made more terrible by the magical swirling symbols on his skin and the lime or chalk paste stiffening his hair which creates an illusion of added height. Around his neck and wrists are bracelets and a torque, which he may have taken as trophies of war from a vanquished foe. In his mind is the desire to take the head of his next great opponent, in order to preserve it and display it reverently in his roundhouse. In the years that follow he will show it off, telling the tale to awestruck listeners of how he took the head of a once mighty warrior and came to possess the home of his very soul.

This ritualised code of conduct on the battlefield would continue even if no opposing champion came forward. Once the battle had started, the champion would probably still choose his opponents by virtue of their apparent importance or prowess, and therefore continue to fight for his own personal glory. With the battle then won the champion could return back to his home and, at the victory feast, claim the warrior's portion as he drank heavily and boasted loudly of the great men he had slaughtered on the field that day. Ultimately the desire of the individual champion to demonstrate his credentials as a great and powerful warrior was no doubt the downfall of many a Celtic army. Many lost battles against Roman forces as discipline and the team ethos of the legions repeatedly prevailed over their less organised foe. Because of this deeply rooted notion of the conduct demanded in warfare, it seems that the tribes of Britain would always struggle to defeat an army such as that of Rome.

FIGURE H. THE VEXILLATION FORTRESS AT MANCETTER (MANDUESSEDUM)

Although the existence of a large, first-century AD Roman fortification at Mancetter is certain, what is less certain is the layout and purpose of the fortress. There is also no certainty as to the exact dates during which it was in use or the various roles for which it was intended during its lifetime.

The reconstructed image shown here seeks to offer a possible interpretation of the information gleaned since the first explorations of the military site at Roman Mancetter began in 1955. Since that time a picture has slowly started to emerge of a large-scale fortification covering some twenty-five acres (ten hectares) and measuring around 1,080 by 1,010 feet (330 by 310 metres). The image is also a visualisation of a theoretical usage for the fort, based on its possible role at the time of the Boudican revolt.

The illustration shows the fortress as viewed from the north, almost directly above where Watling Street would be running west towards Shropshire and the Welsh border. The River Anker traces its way through the foreground, providing a natural defensive barrier for the eastern defences of the fortress, echoing the manner in which the great legionary fortress at Exeter faces the river Exe and the Longthorpe vexillation fortress looks out to the River Nene. To the rear of the western defences the land rises into a thickly wooded slope, and in the distant south lies the area suggested by Webster as the site of the decisive battle between Boudica and Paulinus.

The fortress itself is skirted by a defensive system of double ditches fronting a turf and timber defensive rampart. Archaeological evidence has suggested that the ditch system extended down the slope towards the Anker, making sense of the common view that the fortress faced back towards the east. These defences may have been augmented by the use of stake barriers and sharpened branches driven into the outer faces of the turf ramparts. This orientation may provide a clue as to the earliest phases of the fortress's life, given that such bases were normally constructed to face the threat they were intended to counter. This may therefore indicate that Ostorius Scapula had the fortress built as a direct response to the threat posed during the first Icenian revolt in AD 47.

Since its earliest phase of existence the fortress may then have undergone several changes of role, as evidenced by the final phase of the life of the site when a dramatic downsizing of the base saw a much smaller auxiliary fort occupying the site prior to the Roman military pulling out completely. It is possible that after being constructed for its primary role, the original fortress then evolved into a rear-area supply depot capable of supporting the governor's advance towards Wales. At that time its location was very close to what was then the Scapulan frontier, as represented by the Fosse Way. In this phase the fortress could have supported the advancing army by gathering in and storing supplies from the pacified areas before despatching them up Watling Street to the forward units.

Once the advancing army had pushed far to the west, the life of the site as a key supply depot would have come to an end. Sites further west along the line of the advance would have then become more important in the line of supply, and subsequently operations at Manduessedum would have been wound down. However, it seems very unlikely, given the turbulent nature of the Roman occupation at the time, and the fort's close proximity to the tactically important junction at High Cross, that its importance would have diminished quite so soon.

It seems more sensible to suggest that the site would have remained an operationally active base and would possibly have housed a caretaker garrison when not hosting a full complement of men. The site would then have acted as an occasional base for a large combined battle group made up of legionary and auxiliary soldiers, able to swiftly deploy along the growing road network in response to any problems. A scenario such as the Boudican revolt would therefore have amply demonstrated the wisdom of such contingency planning, as LEG XIIII made its way back to the site after leaving Wales under Paulinus in AD 61.

The suggested layout shows a fortress capable of housing the first cohort of LEG XIIII. This is shown by the larger extended barrack blocks with slightly bigger centurions' quarters next to the *principia* building located at the centre of the site. There is sufficient accommodation for around 2,400 legionaries and a quingenary part-mounted auxiliary cohort, with stabling in the western half of the site for the cavalry mounts. A large and spacious praetorium building is included which would adequately accommodate the legion's legate. In addition, seven granaries, numerous store buildings and workshops attest to the site's former role as a supply depot.

The layout shown is of course mostly speculative, and given that much of the site now lies beneath a densely built-up area, one can only theorise as to the detailed nature of the site. However, in the context of the arguments presented within this work, the layout and usage suggested would seem to be the most appropriate.

APPENDIX 2

ORGANISATIONAL STRUCTURE OF THE ROMAN LEGION, FIRST CENTURY AD

Contubernium	8 men
Century	10 contubernia (80 men)
Cohort I (Manipular Strength)	5 double centuries (800 men)
Cohorts II–IX	6 centuries per cohort (480 men)
Mounted scouts and despatch riders	120 men
Total combat strength	5,240 men
(excluding non-combatant staff)	

TYPICAL LEGION BATTLE LINE: ORDER OF COHORTS

1st line COH V – COH IV★ – COH III – COH II★ – COH I
2nd line COH X – COH IX★ – COH VIII – COH VII★ – COH VI

★ Denotes cohorts of less experienced troops, with VII and IX probably containing the legion's newest recruits. This order of battle ensures that the stronger units lend support to the weaker, inexperienced ones while the formation containing the legion's finest troops, Cohort I, is first into battle.

APPENDIX 3

TABLE OF DISTANCES BETWEEN KEY LOCATIONS, WITH MARCHING TIMES

From	To	Imperial miles	Km	Roman miles	Normal pace*	Forced march*
Lincoln	Colchester	150.1	241.6	163.2	8.1 days	6.5 days
Longthorpe	Colchester	94.3	151.7	102.5	5.1 days	4.1 days
Thetford	Colchester	43.7	70.3	47.5	2.3 days	1.9 days
Caistor St Edmund	Colchester	57.8	93	62.8	3.1 days	2.5 days
Colchester	London	65	104.5	70.6	3.5 days	2.8 days
London	St Albans	24.5	39.4	26.6	1.3 days	1 day

Anglesey	Wroxeter	90.2	145.2	98.1	4.9 days	3.9 days
Anglesey	Wall	135.6	218.3	147.5	7.3 days	5.9 days
Anglesey	Mancetter	157	252.7	170.7	8.5 days	6.8 days
Anglesey	London	256.4	412.6	278.7	13.9 days	11.1 days
London	High Cross	90.7	146	98.6	4.9 days	3.9 days
St Albans	High Cross	68.6	110.5	74.6	3.7 days	2.9 days
St Albans	Leicester	79.2	127.5	86.1	4.3 days	3.4 days

* Normal pace is defined as 20 Roman miles per day.
* Forced march is defined as 25 Roman miles per day.

All distances have been calculated using modern routes, in order to avoid the errors which are likely to occur when attempting to predict the location of now missing sections of Roman road. All distances shown are therefore to be regarded as approximate only.

BIBLIOGRAPHY AND FURTHER READING

MODERN REFERENCE WORKS

Adkins, R. & L., *Dictionary of Roman Religion*. Facts on File Inc., New York, 1996.

Allen, Stephen, *Celtic Warrior 300 BC–AD 100*. Osprey, Oxford, 2001.

Barrett, John C., P.W.M. Freeman and Ann Woodward, *Cadbury Castle Somerset, the Later Prehistoric and Early Historic Archaeology*. English Heritage, London, 2000.

Beresford Ellis, Peter, *The Celts: a Brief History*. Robinson, London, 2003.

Collingridge, Vanessa, *Boudica*. Ebury Press, London, 2005.

Collingwood, R.G., and R.P. Wright, *The Roman Inscriptions of Britain (RIB)*, Vol. I: *Inscriptions on Stone*. Sutton Publishing, Stroud, 1984.

Connolly, Peter, *Greece and Rome at War*. MacDonald & Co., London, 1981.

De La Bedoyere, Guy, *Defying Rome. The Rebels of Roman Britain*. Tempus, Stroud, 2003.

Drummond-Murray, James, and Peter Thompson, *Settlement in Roman Southwark – Archaeological Excavations (1991–98) for the London Underground Ltd Jubilee Line Extension Project* (Monograph 12). Museum of London Archaeology Service, London, 2002.

Frere, S.S., and J.K. St Joseph, *Britannia*, Vol. V: *The Roman Fortress at Longthorpe*. Society for the Promotion of Roman Studies, London, 1974.

Frere, S.S., and R.S.O. Tomlin, *The Roman Inscriptions of Britain (RIB)*, Vol. II: *Instrumentum Domesticum*. Sutton Publishing, Stroud, 1995.

Gilliver, C.M., *The Roman Art of War*. Tempus, Stroud, 2001.

Green, Miranda J. (ed.), *The Celtic World*. Routledge, London, 1995.

Hazel, John, *Who's Who in the Roman World*. Routledge, London, 2001.

Hingley, Richard, and Christina Unwin, *Boudica, Iron Age Warrior Queen*. Hambledon & London, London, 2005.

Peddie, John, *Conquest, the Roman Invasion of Britain*. Sutton Publishing, Stroud, 1987.

Robinson, H. Russell, *The Armour of Imperial Rome*. Arms & Armour Press (Lionel Leventhal), London, 1975.

Roman Britain, Historical Map & Guide (5th ed.). Ordnance Survey, Southampton.

Ross, Ann, and Don Robins, *The Life and Death of a Druid Prince*. Guild Publishing, London, 1989.

Sealey, Paul R., *The Boudican Revolt against Rome* (2nd ed). Shire Publications, Princes Risborough, 2004.

Standing, G., *Britannia*, Vol. XXXVI: *The Varian Disaster & the Boudican Revolt*. Society for the Promotion of Roman Studies, London, 2005.

Sumner, Graham, *Roman Military Clothing (1): 100 BC–AD 200*. Osprey, Oxford, 2002.

Taylor, J., *Northamptonshire Extensive Urban Survey, Whilton lodge (Bannaventa)*. Northamptonshire County Council, 2002.

Taylor, J., G. Foard *et al.*, *Northamptonshire Extensive Urban Survey (Towcester)*. Northamptonshire County Council, 2002.

Webster, Graham, *The Roman Imperial Army of the First & Second Centuries AD* (3rd ed.). University of Oklahoma Press, 1998.

—, *Boudica, the British Revolt against Rome AD 60*. Routledge, London, 1999.

—, *The Roman Invasion of Britain*. Routledge, London, 1999.

Warry, John, *Warfare in the Classical World*. Salamander, London, 1980.

Watson, G.R., *The Roman Soldier*. Cornell University Press, New York, 1969.

Woolliscroft, D.I., *Roman Military Signalling*. Tempus, Stroud, 2001.

CLASSICAL SOURCES

Cassius Dio, *The Roman Histories*.

Josephus, *The Jewish Wars*.

Julius Caesar, *The Gallic Wars*.

Pliny the Elder, *Natural History*.

Suetonius, *The Twelve Caesars*.

Tacitus, *Annals of Imperial Rome*.

—, *The Agricola*.

—, *The Histories*.

QUICK REFERENCE WEBSITES

http://reference.allrefer.com/encyclopedia/categories/ahistrombio.html
http://www.ospreypublishing.com/content2.php/cid=206
http://www.morien-institute.org/morienbiog.html
http://penelope.uchicago.edu/Thayer/E/home.html
http://www.roman-britain.org/main.htm
http://www.wikepedia.org/
http://www.rentaroman.co.uk

PLACES OF INTEREST

The British Museum
Great Russell Street
London
WC1B 3DG
Tel. 0207 323 8000
www.thebritishmuseum.ac.uk

Butser Ancient Farm (address & numbers for enquiries)
Nexus House
Gravel Hill
Waterlooville
Hampshire
PO8 0QE
Tel. 023 9259 8838
www.butser.org.uk

The Castle Museum
High Street
Colchester
Essex

Tel. 01206 282939
www.colchestermuseums.org.uk

The Jewry Wall Museum and Site
St. Nicholas Circle
Leicester
LE1 4LB
Tel. 0116 225 4971
www.leicestermuseums.ac.uk

The Museum of London
London Wall
London
EC2Y 5HN
Tel. 0207 600 0807
www.themuseumoflondon.org.uk

National Roman Legion Museum
High Street
Caerleon
Newport
NP18 1AE
Tel. 01633 423 134
www.museumwales.org.uk

Iceni Royal Enclosure (site of), Thetford
The enclosure is north of the Fison's Way Industrial Estate, off Mundford
Road. Gallows Hill itself can be seen at the junction of the A134 and the
A11 bypass.

Iceni Village & Museums
Swaffham
PE37 8AG
Tel. 017660 721339

Venta Icenorum (site of)
5 km south of Norwich city centre, 800 metres south of Norwich
southern bypass (A47), grid reference TG234034. There is a car park
south of the site.

Verulamium Museum
St. Michael's Street
St. Albans
Hertfordshire
AL3 4SW
Tel. 01727 751810
www.stalbansmuseums.org.uk

Wroxeter Roman City
Wroxeter
Shrewsbury
Shropshire
SY5 6PH
Tel. 01743 761330
www.english-heritage.org.uk

ACKNOWLEDGEMENTS

I would firstly like to extend my special thanks to my former contubernium mate, Brett Thorn, County Archaeologist for Buckinghamshire, for his professional support and guidance from the very start of this project and for supplying me with numerous suggestions and research leads, all of which have contributed greatly to the final content of this work.

I am also indebted to Helen Wells, Assistant Planning Archaeologist and SMR officer for Leicestershire County Council, for supplying me with a wealth of archaeological data relating to the area of High Cross. Her prompt and efficient turnaround of my many requests for information was indispensable in building a case for the area as the possible site of the battle.

My sincerest thanks are also due to John Smith, curator of Bignor Roman Villa, West Sussex. His unconditional offer of help and support was gratefully received and, as someone previously unknown to me, he provided me with the assurance of an unbiased and, as it transpired, very thorough proof-reading of the original manuscript. His suggested amendments subsequently gave me the confidence to submit the completed manuscript and the help and support he has offered since then has been greatly appreciated.

Finally, I would like to extend my sincerest thanks to the following individuals and organisations who have contributed to this work by way of their time, effort, and expertise:

Chris Addison, Historic Environment Record Officer for Northamptonshire County Council.
City of London Sites and Monuments Records Office.
Department of Archaeology, Colchester Museum, Colchester.
Dr Mick Jones, Archaeologist for the City of Lincoln.
Ben Robinson, Archaeological Officer for the City of Peterborough.
Christine Shaw, Butser Ancient Farm, Hampshire.
Ben Wallace, Assistant Historic Environment Record Officer, Warwickshire County Council.

AUTHOR'S NOTE

While mentioning certain archaeological features around the area of High Cross which may indicate Roman military activity, I have been deliberately obscure as to their location where possible. Although I have indicated the possible presence of a low defensive earthwork, I have chosen not to include indications as to the whereabouts of two possible Roman marching camps in the area. I have also decided that certain other features which I found to be of interest during my research should not be included within this work.

High Cross is an important archaeological site, and in order to preserve areas that have not yet been investigated I have omitted specific details such as photographs and other material that may reveal their location. While this may prove a disappointment to genuinely interested readers who would wish to review further supporting evidence, I would hope that, despite the inconvenience, they understand the motivations behind my decision to withhold any material that I believe may threaten the archaeology of the area.

John Waite, 1 February 2006.

LIST OF ILLUSTRATIONS

All illustrations and photographs are the work of the author.

INDEX